fe and it's service brands, including Glasgow

The Bright Tethers
Poems 1988–2016

David Cameron

Rún
PRESS

POCKET POEMS

For Louise

Published in 2016 by Rún Press Limited, Cork, Ireland.

www.runepress.ie

Printed and bound in Great Britain by
TJ International Ltd., Padstow, Cornwall.

Typeset by Stephen Cameron, Glasgow, Scotland

ISBN: 978-0-9574669-6-8

Contents

Love at First

Loss x 2

Victory and Liquorice

The Stranger

And After All

The Temple Monster:

M

Night Singing

An Attic Room on Rose Street

INTRODUCTION

This is the first collection of poems by David Cameron, who was born in Glasgow in 1966. Cameron has been dedicated to poetry all his life. He has said that when he first began to read books, 'I saw that poems spoke about things that weren't ordinarily spoken about.' One event that could not be 'ordinarily' spoken about may have been the death of his father George Cameron following a road accident when bicycling to work: both he and his wife Mary (née McDade) were industrial chemists residing in a suburb of Glasgow, East Kilbride. George Cameron's family were originally from a Gaelic speaking area of the Highlands, and his mother's family were from Tyrone and Sligo in Ireland. His father, originally Protestant, had converted to Catholicism, and the McDades were Catholic, so Cameron was brought up as a Catholic.

Cameron has been writing poems since his early teens, but 'kept poems under wraps' in his early twenties until he sent some to Martin Seymour-Smith who replied that he was 'a real poet', and as Cameron puts it 'provided the affirmation I sought'. This seems to have been enough. Cameron does not hawk his poems around much – although he has found publishers for a novella and short stories, *Rousseau Moon* (2000), and for a literary crime novel, *The Ghost of Alice Fields* (2014), and he has written reviews and had poems published in a dozen or so periodicals. He won the Hennessy Literary Award for Poetry in Ireland in 2014, and that year he edited and introduced *The Poems of Martin Seymour-Smith*.

The Camerons (the name in Gaelic means the Crooked-noses) and the McDades (the 'sons of David') may be said to be clans, but this Cameron belongs to no clan: he is one of the most independent-minded men I know. He has never worked for an institution. After university in Aberdeen (where he began in English Literature and ended in Social Anthropology) he worked briefly in a fish factory and a dairy, then as a care assistant in a 'hospital school' for Epilepsy in Surrey. Later he lived and wrote in a cottage 'underlooking' the Forth Bridge in Edinburgh, then he moved to Amsterdam where his wife Louise Rice studied glass art. In Amsterdam, Cameron worked as a language tutor, then as a writer-editor for the European Cultural Foundation (ECF). For some years the Camerons lived in Leitrim where he continued working on a freelance basis for the ECF, and since 2015 they have lived in Northern Ireland where he works as a learning consultant.

Cameron does not make a living from literature, and certainly not from poetry. He goes out to work, in one world or another, and he sells his ideas and his skills, but he will never sell his soul. And as an editor he works with words: his poems are spontaneous and inspired, then carefully crafted. He lives an ordinary and unassuming life as a family man, and many of his poems are about ordinary things, but they are not ordinary poems. He sees from a different angle – the poet's angle. He is not only, as Seymour-Smith put it, 'a real poet', he is a real person – and has been called by at least one friend 'the real David Cameron'.

I have known Cameron since we started corresponding in 1998. Whether playing football with children, or talking humorously as he washes the dishes or on walks along the sea, or over a drink, there is something serious about him – in the old sense of being consistent across any 'series' of events. I trust his judgment. And it is hard won. He thinks for himself. Whether these poems are light-hearted or heavy-hearted, the reader will take them seriously.

Cameron cares about being a father – to his own children and, I suspect, to himself. Some people who grow up without a father get stuck in seeking for a father in others. Cameron finds a father in himself. Some of these poems are about fathers and sons. Others are about passions and fears. The changing landscapes of Cameron's emotions, and of his lives in Scotland, Holland, and Ireland permeate these poems. They are about what IS. They contain few generalisations, and no 'shoulds'.

Cameron does not teach poetry or write essays about it, but he is as curious as any inspired poet about 'what poetry is'. His way of exploring this is in his stories and novels, especially the unpublished *Femke*, in which a young woman in Amsterdam becomes the executor of a dying poet, De Koning. The series of 12 sonnets in this collection which end the section 'M' are written 'as' De Koning, and in the novel *Femke*, De Koning may be writing them 'as' someone else. Who writes a poem? Where does it come from? How does it come from nowhere to move the writer as well as the reader? The writer is the first reader of the poem.

As the first reader, Cameron works carefully on his poems. But what strikes me most is their capacity to surprise me. They have clearly surprised him. (Given his high standards for poetry, he would not have written them otherwise). Cameron has remarked that some of the De Koning poems, written as it were in a voice not his own, moved him to tears. Some of the poems in this extraordinarily varied collection have moved me to tears also. Others make me smile. Many make me wonder about life and death. All of them add something to my sense of the world.

Seán Haldane

AUTHOR'S NOTE

This is the book I have been writing all my life, and that all my life has been writing. The first poem here is from 1988, but I wrote my first poem almost a decade earlier, at the age of 12 – and the theme of that one reached further back into my childhood. At 12 I was as suspicious of poetry as most people are, so the poem came as a surprise: a sudden revelation, but of something I realised I had always known.

That first poem was plain to understand, traditional in its rhythms, full of feeling, and about my mother. Soon afterwards I wrote a different kind of poem: cryptic, 'experimentally' structured according to sound, full of feeling, and about my dead father. The cryptic style won out for several years – it was as if unconscious matter was erupting but not yet flowing into consciousness.

In time I learned about poetry as a craft, as (arguably) an art form. But it was the involuntary, electrifying experience of writing those first poems that stayed with me as guide. It's the unlooked-for poem that I trust.

As this is not only a collected poems but also my first collection of poems, I have decided to arrange the poems thematically rather than (confusingly) chronologically, though there is a rough chronology within each section.

I am grateful for the advice of a number of readers of my poems over the years, and especially to my friend since university days, Iain MacDonald, to Seán Haldane and the late Robert Nye, and to my wife Louise Rice.

David Cameron

Love at First

ROSARY

In the month of May,
In the depths of my old school,
The corridors were lined
With acquiescent girls –
Some in chapel veils –
As well as the odd boy.
Along the stringed beads
The nimble fingers moved,
The nimble fingers which
I daily ached to touch.

In that hour before the bell,
I was possessed by all
The murmuring and clacking,
The concentrated air
Of girls – some of them veiled! –
Caught up in adoration.
And though, in truth, I could
Have done with the extra sleep,
The thick stupor of prayer
Only strengthened my desire

For one among them there.

VALENTINES

He bought his love a box of Roses.
'That is so sweet,' the two girls chimed,
Their different heads, brunette and blonde,
Meeting above the opened box.
'Hazel in Caramel!' 'Strawberry Dream!'

Well, yes, I thought, *but mine will be
Sweeter still.* 'What have you got
Dearer than Roses, not too dear?'
The woman smiled above the till.

Terry's All Gold! A penny more!
If what the advert said was true,
When I lifted her desk lid, left
The box containing all my hope,
And after playtime watched to catch
Her blonde hair, her brilliant teeth
Reflected in its purest gold –
I'd see the face I loved light up.

'But I don't like dark chocolate.'

I knew, she didn't have to say,
'Not to me they're not,'
When I said they were dearer than Roses.

LOVE AT FIRST

If the hook-hung, wet duffel bag
Came back to shred my chest again,
I would keep all whole. I would keep
Knees bent to break now-fearless falls.
It would be different this time.
This time, in good time, I would go
Strong-nerved to meet my Waterloo:
You.

CARNIVAL EVENING

1

She handed him the letter, said: 'Burn this.'
The bearded man by the bandstand
Was suddenly at the bridge.
She kept saying, 'I don't want this moon,'
Went home, wept, slept, her strange house dream
Tormenting her, filling her up,
Till its jerking, drugged puppet appeared.

2

She must fix precisely the location,
Mark the hill trees bordering the dark,
The blonde tree-fire of the moon,
The night scene they walked trembling into.
It must be clear to her, clearer
With every guessing second, how it was:
What that betrayal meant and means now

– Hers of him

By the side road, next to the high tower.

A FACE

A face in the distorting rope-held mirror,
Almost forgotten, *her* face
(The face that owned your teenage love):
Describe this face.

A red light in an attic room is better.

It brings back
Desires you don't quite hate and don't quite lack.

YOUNG LOVE

Above the smoke
That rises from our cigarette
Her ceiling's yellowing and bare
Till curious misshapen heads
Appear there.

When she was called
Into the kitchen, had *the truth*
Prised out of her, I didn't doubt –
Running my hand along her side –
She'd lied.

She likes to curl
Up into a ball and play
Music methodically to the end,
Then clean the needle choked with dust
From our lust.

RUINS

1
On an old dial
My young hand calls you up.
I'm ready, I say, I'm set.

From the most known
To streets that spread like a disease
O all the way to your door.

And there is mum and dad and dog,
And sister gone before us
Down the dark road we'd take.

2
Sweet Jane *is on the radio,*
On your turntable going slow.
Sweet Jane *is all around.*
Sweet, sweet Jane.

I never hung around
In underpasses; won't start now
Graffitiing your name.
I will always be the same.

You know I won't say love
Except to say I don't, not you,
Not even after this.
And if this isn't love, what is?

3
Stairs
That make you turn in a space –
Will the air there
Hold your body's jasmine
For me?

Axis,
Arrow that all along
Wanted to find you,
Wanted to coat its head
With your blood.

4
Of the kittens that were found abandoned
O over the moors
We choose the most frightened.

Your sister's gift.
Now puncture holes
In the cardboard, make her comfortable.
I'll take her on the bus, in a yellow light.

O over the moors.
If you're young
It's where they murder you, I learned.

Now there's a living thing between us
We're fixed like this forever.
Wrap her up in your headscarf,

Stroke her and purr the words
That are meant for me.
But in her eyes the fear won't go.
The wilderness in us is what they show

O.

5
I think in fact you don't have on her dress
And I'm not wading through the mist,
But your letter is yellow,

The branches unimaginably green.
It's useless, you say, we're dying:
If someone's there in hiding, let him see.

We're not like animals,
We know our fate too soon.
I have no crow to pluck with you, my friend.

Your room your refuge,
But I feel better here
In ruins where a different moon will rise.

DOWN-A-DOWN

Where the wires cross, I saw
Trouble on her brow,
Along her jaw,
Loss in her eyes.
I caught a feather from her hat,
Said: 'I'm with you now.'

As she hit the ground,
I heard her moan –
A yellow sound,
A wounded horn's –
'I'm a careless acrobat
I know. Leave me alone.'

Once she called me the floundering one
On a wet fire escape in the sun.

SORROW IN TIME

1
Not so fast, Barrel Man.
Slow your organ down.
I think I heard my life in it
About a minute back.

And there it is again,
More strained, less faint this time:
The same schmaltzy tune,
Forgotten, known by heart.

Speed up, speed up.
A face on your warped wood
Reminds me there is someone
I have to warn in time.

2
'Let me come into the storm,'
A wilful, flame-haired girl
Sings in a stink of jasmine;
Makes room for me on the bed.
After, in icy streets,
Our kettle-breath comes quick.
Why is she standing now,
Head bowed, by a rowan tree?

THE ANTIDOTE

'Christ,' she said, 'it was just a year ago
You and your mum watched *Dallas*, eating chocolate.'
I'm grateful now for what that redhead brought:
The antidote to comfort. Love and hate,
Or not quite hate, seemed intertwined back then.
Her coffee tasted bitter, I remember;
Wherever I stood felt like a cliff-edge.
It put me in mind of one bleak, dark December.
And that's how my life has gone, my head resting
On a warm bosom and then a cold rock,
Wanting both simultaneously, half
In hate of softness, half in love with shock.
The thrill of this is felt not just by me.
The price of this is paid not just by me.

WALLPAPER

There is music on the stairs.
'Concentrate!' she calls. It's true
I'm here stripping wallpaper,
Wishing I was stripping you.
And somehow it's you singing,
As the double bass beats time
More languidly than my pulse,
Is it a sin? Is it a crime?
Well, if I can get through this
In a morning, rush the job,
I'll find a quiet corner
And dream of you. Then what? Sob?
My heart's with the wallpaper paste
Congealing in a plastic bucket:
It will never sing to you;
It will never...
          Ah, fuck it.
Life's too short for sin or crime
To be the touchstone of desire.
Better these papered walls burn down –
I'll take my chances in the fire.

GREEN ONIONS

'I have to tell you that she hasn't aged well.
Bereft of good looks and manners, she drinks
To absolute excess …'

I was, in memory, thirteen,
She three years above me,
Though school was not my playground
Of desire. The village hall
Had a Sunday disco. I eyed her there
Week after week, until, *Green Onions* playing,
I walked up, said the words I'd long rehearsed
And she smiled yes. I threw myself into it
While she, well, barely moved her feet.

Whenever I hear the track,
Whenever I slice green onions,
I see that girl, her eyes,
Her smirk, her slanting feet,
And I am back
In that wooden hut –
For three wordless minutes
The universe's centre –
At the mercy of my crush.

BOOK LOVE

Was ours a boy-and-girl-type love,
As in Hemingway's shortest story?
Was it censorable, like Ulysses?
Could it be read on Jackanory?
Were you Rebecca, scoffing, fierce,
Or the second Mrs de Winter?
Was I cute-naughty, drawn by Potter,
Or a sinister out of Pinter?
Romance began, middled, and ended
And there was no second edition.
We were Li Po/Pound's 'Two small people
Without dislike or suspicion.'

THE HURT

I arrived heroically,
Like Lenin at Finland Station,
Every fourth Friday,
Clutching my little holdall.
Hungover on Hanover Street,
I'd remember the present
I never managed to give
– The one acquired by magic:
That just-so, real, true gift.
I made the shop doors chime
Right the way down Dundas Street
Where the antiques and rarities
Cost more than I could afford.
And so it was I landed,
Face flushed, on your doorstep,
Myself my only gift
– Which you duly unwrapped
On long weekends in bed
(Clothed, we made necessary
Forays into the kitchen
When nobody seemed about).
Into that fond world
I brought – another death.
I swore it was as if
Faith could only be proved
By infidelity.
And though I still don't know,
But can guess, the hurt caused,
I know I caused the hurt.

WEEKEND IN THE COUNTRY

The smell of your place – the dampness, is it?
Or hash (not yours, I know), or maybe incense –
The smell is still, a week after my visit,
Thick in my clothes. These clothes that I wore once
Not thinking anything, I can't put on
Without saying your name. And I do say it.

I know, I know, you were right in that letter
You sent afterwards, about it not being love.
I caught you at a low point (but you're better).
You're right to stress this too. I'm not above
Nudging in, exploiting the occasion:
We know it, both of us, to our pleasure.

You've got a good life there. Don't spoil it.
The animals, a cottage in the country;
The location, too – I really loved it.
Sooner throw a weekend than a life away.
All that talk, we were having each other on.
Old, old feelings. And I can't forget it.

POST

Your letter arrived, saying
I should be forgiving.
I would forgive you, dear,
If it ended there.
What's unforgiven, though,
(Will always be so)
Is that flat passionless tone
Nauseating to the bone.

SOMETIMES THE SUMMER

Sometimes the summer appears
In other seasons; as, today,
I was settling down to winter
When it began.

So I walk across the fields, collecting the years,
Summers that have been, and meet you there,
Eyes glinting like sails, last year.
Thank you. I want never again
To settle into winter like snow.
Here are the same fields and fences,
The earth that will invite the lambs to dance,
Water with something clear to say.

THE LONGEST ROUTE

Because there is a light in the window,
Bodies upstairs preparing for day,
I do not go as I normally go,
Twirling a stick or tapping it on my way
As if to divine a mystery.

I take the longest route from A to B
And only stop to flip a stone over:
There is damp earth, nothing else to see.
My dear, I have been dead this past year;
So much so, you could call me your stone lover.

I shout: I'm too young to be an effigy.
But did stone speak, I'd hear the hills replying:
Younger than you are now you learned to say,
'Why are you crying?
What is wrong? Why am I dying?'

THE SHEET

The rest is silence.
How you floated away from me
Up through the air, into outer space.
I struggled against the sheet that was wrapped round me;
Cursed you asleep, but I had made the bed.

You're back and out of breath,
Hair caught in the side of your mouth.
Behind my eyes I ran the length and breadth
Of England to meet my friend travelling south.
How far does he suspect that I am dead?

The squirrels master air
And bend the branches outside the window.
You have just left. It is unfair
That family cry more for you when you go.
The sheet that is wrapped round me is made of lead.

DECEMBER SNOWS

We belong to each other much more
During December snows.
Snow is trailed through the open door,
And the trail we left outside grows and grows.

I lift the fresh pineapple juice –
It is so cold also.
I don't bother that the latch is loose,
In case tomorrow there is no snow.

The children are building a snowman
With their imaginations.
They send us away. Well, if they can,
Let them do better than we did with simple things.

PORTENT

The sun now
Indistinguishable from cloud
(Soon it is no more than a spot):
I say that the sun has set.
But you, gypsy-like,
As if reading a portent there,
Make out a headless bird in the red air.

PRIMROSES

Audible with a shout
And visible as pain,
From Boghead Bridge to Diamond Lane
All the primroses are out.

Having eaten a vaseful's
A good reminder. 'It's true,'
You say, 'they're good for you,
Even the petals.'

So tonight we'll go
Up the black hill and explore,
And you will show me once more
Country things I didn't know.

Incredibly, I asked you what
Colour a primrose was. The ones
I know are childhood's: dandelions,
Flowers that are less picked than caught.

I am not good on life
Exactly, and at Boghead Bridge
I saw no flowers but a knife
Lying flat on its blunt edge.

LUCKY

It's lucky, you said,
You ate the primrose
As a child and not
The poisonous crocus.

What stopped you then
Was a playful instinct
We consider now,
Our long fingers linked.

Why do we have to grow
Old together?
Your look dares me to eat
The poison flower.

WILDERNESS

'Is this wilderness enough for you?'
She points out wild flowers, names them. It's dark
Despite the sun, in the narrowing avenue
Of trees, 'a shivery wee lane'. Pollok Park
In summer, and small families go floating past
Pollok House, the Burrell, and the river.
She scrutinises the lane with fast
Turns of thought – 'I'd like a horse to come down here,
I mean me coming down here on a horse' –
And bends to the water. As a girl, she sent
Flowers like this downstream, with as little force.
'Where did they go? I don't know where they went.'
Envying her country ways, I ask can we go.
'They probably sank,' she says, 'I don't want to know.'

I KNOW, I KNOW

We have to live,
I know, except
At times it seems
A secret best kept.

I know we have to,
And like you I cling
To a time when it seemed like
The very dearest thing.

LEAVING

You buckled up your leather case
(Stylish, though we were always poor),
Made your way straight before my face,
Like the long path of Fala Moor.

I studied trains, the forlorn cross
(A blasted tree against the sky);
Not desolate, I thought: *No loss.*
She's leaving me. I won't die.

A mind-dark kitchen, plate of fruit …
The images rebound in me
From that day still, though not the route
I walked and walked and couldn't see.

OLD MOVIES

Old movies in the afternoon
We don't so readily dismiss:
They feed our feelings with a spoon.
Improbables undressed to kiss

– Or only partly, a wrap, a shoe,
Enough to signify undress.
I keep my clothes on, so do you.
Nice if we can avoid distress.

Domesticity never was
Our strong point, and we failed to find
Redeeming traits revealed through use.
Though not entirely unkind,

Love has gnawed us to the bone.
Yet the thought plagues you, confess,
That self-discovered and alone
You'll be content with nothing less.

FUTURE

All on an April morning
Sun split the cloud, revealed
Two crouching, touching, talking
In a barley field.

'Our future's ours to see.
I see it like my dream
Of Chinese shacks, us huddled,
Our breath a stream.

Exotic, even if poor.'
'I see it differently.
The same: us huddled,
Not like today.

I see us poor and huddled
Just in the way you meant,
Against, but against each other
In our hearts' tenement.'

'What sawest thou, that thou hast done this thing?'

What was it you saw, that made you do this?
Did your own shadow rise to frighten you,
The earth split between your feet? What, then?
I walk barefoot, a caged beast in a zoo,
The same floorboards, thinking I could murder you.

You'll have your reasons worked out to a T,
If I know you. I knew you. Say one:
My breath stinks, maybe my shirt's unironed,
Or else you dreamt I ran off with some woman;
You're remembering you're an enemy of man.

Remembering my Homer, I face my grief
By eating my supper up like a good boy,
And do the usual things, like open the door
When someone calls for me. You won't destroy
The machine me, the me like a clockwork toy.

All day I ravel and unravel my thoughts.
My only peace is watching for the heron
To fly back and settle in the river
When it's night again, and the orange streetlights are on,
And I stand and am as still as the heron.

ANOTHER DAY

Holidaymakers at play
On a beach in Santorini.
'You were with her, weren't you?'
– That was such another day,
No harm now to say.

And what could have turned out well
Shifts to grey, and worse than grey,
On a bed of volcanic sand
On a beach in Santorini.

NETTLES

Nettles, my boyhood's bane,
Were the shape of evil,
With rumpled-looking dock leaves
Always at hand to heal.

Yes, I was adamant
They would be found together,
Until a stung friend said:
'I don't see dock leaves here.'

How to tell them apart,
Pain and relief from pain,
With no help from nature?
Love is my manhood's bane.

ADDRESSES

1
I met my love on Chestnut Row.
Woken early and told to go,
I walked the streets still flushed with lust,
Contemplating her disgust.

2
In Jute Street, loving my neighbour,
I could sleep but not sleep with her.
The once-born and the born-again
Saw eye to eye in time. Amen.

3
I took a love that seemed complete
And mashed it on McLennan Street;
Endured the dark night of my soul;
Wrapped the clothes line round the clothes pole.

4
Expecting friendship in Boat Green,
I found my Indian-summer queen;
Prepared for her a deli-spread
She ate perched on my single bed.

5
And perched above this last address,
The new Old Orchard's appleless.
We came here of our own free will,
Firstborn in tow, from Edenville.

Loss x 2

YOUR DEATH

It wasn't a hard road, it was a hospital.
The blanket coverage of your death
(We were all tuned in, hanging on every word)
Was wiped out in a snowstorm.
I still remember you
Waving the insects away from my hood
In a dream, clearly.
                    Behind the mirror,
Nothing. Only a thin strip of silver
Kept me from the world you were locked into.
Other worlds than ours, zodiacal signs,
I never trusted in. It doesn't matter,
It never mattered what your star sign was;
That you missed being a bull by just a day;
That the ram's head I doodled in a notebook
Stunned me with fear. I didn't know it then,
Even what day your birthday was.

It was the snow – lying as sleet on bridges,
Still falling through the shock; the snow, numbingly,
Transfiguring the once-known. It was the snow
Which brought down a dream-curtain on the house
And then walled us in. Expect harshness now,
The chained cup of water said, not the snow;
The street flowers and the blue bridge to your grave,
But not the snow, told us what to expect.
Came the thaw, in spring, we walked out to sunshine:
Your death was dandelion seed on the wind.

LOSS x 2

1
Your face was a lynx's, Father,
A comic-surreal lantern
(But the photographs deny it).
You spoke, and spoke out of
A white closet in my dream.
The bass notes ran through my head.

Your watch's marine face broke:
I wanted to smash all portholes.
How could the blue
Bus shelter survive you,
The swing park, the phone?
Why was I looking in the sea for your body
When you died on a hard road?

2
In old wooden furniture
I found secret insignia,
Scratches, hieroglyphs only I could read.

I looked up at houses,
Saw a wheel rolling through the rooms.

What did I love?
The nightwatchman and the open road.
Taking into myself the longing that held him back.

I lit fires, watched smoke move along cold fields.
I looked back at my own absence in the fire.

LYTHAM, ST. ANNE'S

My hat spelled MAVERICK, we sat
In amongst the grasses, Mother.

WHITE BORDERS

Your right hand raised, without its cigarette,
As in a sling, directs the loving eye
Towards my mother's legs, posed touchingly
(In truth, she's not your wife, my mother, yet).

Your smile – not cruel, but wry – has still the ghost
Of jests aimed at the camera-hidden eyes.
Your dark-room negatives survived goodbyes
We never got to say. But we lost most.

I held, as you'd held, slides of foreign places,
Their white borders … Gardens, palace, square.
Found you disembodied, sprawled there:
You in them, and not in any faces.

OUT OF TIME

The curtains blow in no wind, out of time,
Their gold thread pattern not deciphered yet.
Cold on the inside, cold against the glass.

'They took my face away. They changed my hair,
Told me to have it cropped like Joan of Arc.
Spanish-Irish, that would catch a man.

None of them worth it. Shufflers in slacks.
The little painted soldiers on your drum
Are not like anything. Do you understand?'

I understood all right. For me to live
To scream happily in a water flume,
I had to get you out of that dead room.

SURFACES

Cracks in the ceiling troubled me like the growth
On Mum's forehead. I would sit on her lap,
Listening as she sang; drum my stubborn fingers
Towards that growth.

Imperfections on her face
Or imperfections in the house, which was her body,
Set my world to wrongs, mind on its course
To a time when I wanted every surface cracked.

THE ANSWER

'Are my jaws clapped in?' she'd ask
Of the mirror and then me.
'Are they clapped in?' she'd ask,
Meaning: *Answer me! Look at me!*

I thought of old-style lamps
In streets I sleepwalked alone;
Hallucinated iron clamps
From her beauty's bone.

Dismissed them all, said 'No':
The only answer, of course,
Or so I thought.
              – 'You think so?'
'Yes' might not have been worse.

ALL THAT NOW

I liked it when you tucked the blanket round me,
As this was childhood and being sick:
Time when a mother's love was counted on
To discount the playacting laid on thick.

I read my reading book out loud to you.
Words were difficult magic in my tent.
Taught with a finite patience the sound 'then',
I pestered you to spell out what 'then' meant.

I know, it wasn't easy to explain,
And I learned soon enough (easier when
All that contrasts with *now*): at that time, therefore,
And even afterwards. You loved me then.

ALMOST-WEDS
Bundoran

I walk with eyes of pleasure and of awe,
Picturing two familiar almost-weds
Resolved to find new words for what they saw
And never sleep again in separate beds.

In my own eyes a son to them, I'm glad
To walk the same streets – wondering what they said,
In love against a seaside's pale facade –
Not lengths of darkening corridor in my head.

NOTE

Found in a drawer
Of the old Singer sewing machine
Where I sat to write today,
A note
In my mother's handwriting:
'Good luck
On your remaining journey.'
Some part of me knew it was there.

DEAD / IN AMERICA

Snow lands forgetfully
On Winter Palace, factory,
On swings they've long since felled.
Sensing you were 'out there'
In America somewhere,
I yelled.

Red sky to warn the sailors,
But the heavens were all yours:
In death you had your due.
I dodged the pavement cracks,
Dreaming you strolled (shirt open-necked, in slacks)
Fifth Avenue.

RIVAL

Shoe Shuffle Man – in slacks and moccasins,
Sly-eyed and trim –
Disturbed my mum, confused my innocence.
I hated him.

He danced before the crowds on holiday
At Rothesay pier
As piped music struck up mechanically
To greet the steamer.

Forlorn widow, deserving so much better
Than his greased sort
(Charisma-men with hip flasks, doleful patter,
All chasing skirt),

My mum would smile politely and pass on.
I'd turn to stare,
Give him my best Dad-idolising frown.
I saw, years later,

His doppelgänger, filmed emitting charm
At a high retreat,
A swastika emblazoned on one arm;
Same shuffling feet.

ZENO'S PARADOX

Zeno of Elea, I like your saying
No target can be reached by arrow.
My dad's blood never stained a road;
My mum has never tasted sorrow.

ONE MAN'S SONG

1
Of his effects, we had still
A lawnmower but no bicycle.

2
Local Rotarians in their ties
Ran trips for single-parent families.

A sleek Parks of Hamilton bus
Carried off excitable us.

Our urban-rural destination
Was decked out for a celebration.

I'd never seen such happy faces.
We clapped the winners of the races:

Three-legged, egg-and-spoon, and sack.
We gave that pin a fair old whack.

When we got hungry, food was brought
Out from the bus. We scoffed the lot.

Things started to unravel after.
The same games induced less laughter.

I watched the driver check the sky,
As if the weather told him why.

'It's great they went to all this bother,'
The women said to one another.

On the way back some sang a song.
I couldn't help but sing along.

3
I sing a man who went to mow
And mowed himself beneath a meadow.

IN PRAISE OF CARPET BEATERS

My mother urged her mother
To get a carpet beater
When carpet beaters were in fashion.
'It'll take the guts out of the carpet,'
Came back the firm objection.
But a carpet beater was bought, for a daughter
Whose great wish was to be like other women,
Bang up-to-date in 1940s' dress.

From fashion, and a doomed idea of progress,
They took up arms against indoor machines –
Their mothers' dry-rattling Ewbank sweepers –
And beat those carpets mercilessly in back greens.

INVENTORY

Gone is the grass
You cut with the push lawnmower;
Gone are the tools
And the utility room;
Gone from the loft,
The books on mensuration.
Gone is the watch with the bloodied strap.

Gone is the grass
I laid my head on;
Gone are the tools
Puzzled over by these hands;
Gone from the loft,
The poorly hidden presents.
Gone is the ladder with the buckled step.

And still going on:
The wonder at cut grass,
The puzzlement in the hardware store,
The near dread of the loft.
And still going on:
The sudden glance out the window,
The endless waiting for an end
To the wait without hope.

GRIEF

1

The man in the good crombie coat
Is an impostor. Remember,
He is not your father. The coat's
Your father's. Just that. Remember.

2

Why is this house the wrong way round,
And why is it round the wrong way?
In the magnified garden say
Who's afraid of a dog daisy.

3

The milk-white music box has stopped.
The beehive woman on the couch
Smiles as I take a cigarette.
I get to touch each moulded pouch.

4

I do not know which way to turn
The key; if I should come or go.
Is this the door that's just for show?
The lock's in shadow.

HEIRLOOM

My young wife says I am too young
For an old-man dressing gown. She wouldn't
Have me seen dead in one I want.
Which is what, exactly? Nothing my tongue
Can get across, quite. 'A blue-green,
No, green-blue tweed thing, only cottony,
But not towelling; fine-haired, scratchy.
You *know*.' Little wonder she isn't keen.

Then Mum calls, seeing into our lives.
'That old green dressing gown of your father's
Must have been covered in cat hairs.
It's only brought the neighbour out in hives.'
'Get it from the bin, Mum … Just because.'
And so she goes through the bright house, half-blindly,
Now even the cat's dead, and I
Am older than ever my father was.

TO DUST

Expect your expectations to be ground
Down to a grainy dust that they'll call *hope*.
This was the lesson in the cliff for me –
My word for the bank of earth sloping up
From the killer Whirlies. That roundabout,
I told myself, hid what I couldn't find.
My dad, so dear to me, and so forgotten,
Survives still in the almost mindless mind
Of one who got the job his death left vacant.
Take that! life tells you. And of course you do.
It's not what you had hoped for, or expected.
Now find in it one grain of what is true.

AN ACCIDENT

No, Beatrix, it wasn't naughtiness
Propelled young Peter to the very place
His dad became a filling for a pie
– 'An accident', as you so delicately
Put it. And while the others gathered blackberries,
Poor Peter was assailed by friendly sparrows
(He shed big tears; they said 'Exert yourself!')
Bad old McGregor took down from the shelf
A sieve 'to pop upon the top of Peter'
– Who wriggled free, of course. You must know better,
Beatrix; that it wasn't naughtiness
Caused him to long to fill his dear dad's shoes

Or me to wander off from Blackbraes Road
And perch above Rolls-Royce, where Dad had made
Aeroplane engine after aeroplane engine
Until an accident forced all within.

Used for a scarecrow, *his* loss stayed in view –
'A blue jacket with brass buttons, quite new.'

THE GIRL SHE WAS

At a pier-end talent show in Blackpool
I sang Sweet Gypsy Rose. I was slight, yet
Could fairly belt it out. In rehearsal
Mum said: 'Don't just sing. Move your feet a bit.'

And so I belted out Sweet Gypsy Rose
And moved my feet a bit. Had Mum approved?
Her eyes were fixed upon the pointed toes
Of girls doing Irish dancing. This she loved.

Seeing, not those girls, but the girl she was
At a pier-end talent show in Blackpool,
Mum welled up: these were her steps. Knowing this
About her, I felt less of a small fool.

Look, all that's very well, but have you seen her,
Sweet Gypsy, sweet Mary-Jo? I miss her
Now she's joined the burlesque show. Here's her picture.
We were happy. At least, I thought we were.

M&S

To one brought up on a Sligo farm,
Nothing so decadent as this:
The town centre's M&S.

Among the slacks, the pleated skirts,
My gran's errant daughter
Might well have lost herself here.

Tutting from her window seat,
Gran could see through the blinds
The logoed bags in her hands.

I knew where my sympathies lay
In this demure rebellion.
M&S: Mother & Son.

MOVEMENT

I marvelled at her softness – more inferred
Than touched; hid from myself my faint repulsion
At the mothness of her. A devotee
Of clothes-hung spaces, naturally I crept in.

My schoolboy error? Hope of some reward.
As my investigation grew, contempt did too,
And she would be gone for months at a time;
When I smiled or talked to her, gone. It's true

My brightness dazzled, and this drew her nearer –
Not so as to consume her or feed me.
Now, in an unshared darkness, still she moves
Erratically, as I can't fail to see.

TURNS

When I was on the turn
From doting boy to scowling man
My mother's look grew stern.

The look was magnified
By large-eye-rimmed prescription glasses.
I had nowhere to hide.

If either of us could have,
I would have been the one to say
(Her lips being closed to 'love'):

'Whatever else you do,
Love me, although I don't love you –
Or do, while seeming not to.'

But none of that transpired.
And now she's on a turn herself,
I've no clue what's required.

FATHER DEAD

1

Who's that? Who's that at the door
And in my head?
Whatever's said
Makes the day fall away,
Her face go grey.
But it's the eyes I see,
Eyes anxious as a rule, only
Differently today.
Oh this is a different way.

And bundled off, for my own good,
I mirror those eyes for these strangers
Known to me, living
Around the corner in a house like ours,
A house just like ours, only
The wrong way round. In it, a man
Not my father
Looks on helplessly as
The rescued infant rages in his clutch.

2

– What if he doesn't come back?
They say he is on holiday.
They say.
He would take us on holiday.
He would.
Unless he has another family –
Another wife, other sons,
A daughter this time.
In America, they say.

Do they?
Or is that what I say?

Right all along.
Here's the ground he's in.
Past the carriageway,
The factory,
The blue bridge that shakes.
A slim tree beside it
And a wall.
He is there now
Being eaten away, or else
Eaten already.
— What if he comes back?

3
I am in love
With Armitage Shanks.
Don't rip out the bathroom.
Don't change a thing.
Put the tools back
In the tool box —
Not that we can use them anyway —
And put the tool box away.

All right, you can paint,
You can wallpaper,
Just leave the fittings as they are,
And me here
Playing, it seems.
Have you noticed
How in the middle always
I freeze?

4

Not to go mad,
That's the main thing.
In my ripped and oil-stained clothes,
With the branch I call Medicine Stick in my hands,
In my insolence and letters to the press,
I'll be all right, my father says
In a dream.

This girl now
Looks promising
In her ripped and written-on clothes,
Except she doesn't seem the drowning type
Who'll leave me to *not go mad* on my own.
But she does leave. She leaves then comes back,
Then leaves again.

5

Absence the new presence.
How do you like that?
Too slick.
Say it your way, then.
There is no way to say.

Accumulate or decimate?
Try both at once.
The more I have you,
The less there is to love.
Them's the breaks.

6
Just as I was beginning to relent,
To give up the search
For what was never missing,
You turn the tables on me
By looking up at me
Bloodily,
Wordlessly
In a way that spells
Fa-ther.

So I am that for you. I see.
It works like this –
My son found a father.
That father found, found his.
I always would have guessed
Differently,
But that's me

And this is you,
Another story
With undigested morsels of my own –
The gift I bring.

Such eyes I hope you never have to see.

Victory and
Liquorice

TURNING BACK

'I hate turning back on myself,'
I said. 'Is there a different route?'
– Well, it is the expected thing
To say, to think: no turning back,
No going over the same roads,
Except it isn't true, not of me.

I would recover every inch,
Inspect each hedge, commit each hedge
To memory, then forget all
Only to do it all again.

And if you put me into school,
I'll take a book I've read before,
Go to the part I know by heart
Where one cries to another, 'Can't
Repeat the past? Why, of course you can!'

HARLEQUIN

It was the eyes rocked Harlequin.
He ended his game of mirrors, ran
Into the scented night-garden.

The moonlight shifting on the wall:
His brothers' names still legible.
They were no use to him at all.

He looked up. Behind the tree,
His dragon-tree, it slipped away.
There was no She to make it stay.

It is a boy's grief, not Harlequin's.
He's finished with his mirrors, runs
Screaming across the night-gardens.

IN THE CLASSROOM

Indian-maiden-mother,
I have your cotton dress,
Red leather boots,
Your lipstick
Fixed permanently in my head.
Steinbeck, Steinbeck –
Read him to me softly,
Read him to me wantonly
At the edge of the desk.

There is a balm in Gilead,
And in the blood-red
Oranges of my childhood.
Tease it out of me
Slowly – it would be like
Extracting intestines
With toy forceps –
And I'll write them, the only words,
To bebop at full volume.

Sister-mother-wife,
And that other, the redhead
Tying seductively
Her black, black ribbon –
Together in one place!
How I need you there.
But it looks better on me,
This past woven from memory
Of disappearance, absences.

CHANGES

At times a single day
Changes the season.
And so goodbye the summer
After this night of rain.

I've known people to change
Likewise in a moment:
Holding the black receiver,
Jaws clenched, intent.

Eyes I've seen glaze
When asked to look lovingly,
Or else stare into space
Far beyond me

As if into days
Of carpets, children, chairs.
Dead eyes I've seen flicker
At the sight of hares.

At times a single day
Changes the season.
And so goodbye the summer
After this night of rain.

MY FAULT

The seeker turned his back.
You meant not to get caught.
I meant to grow tall
As well as wise for you.
Sorry. Sorry I did not.

The close at Mrs Carr's
Was poor, an afterthought.
The seeker counted short,
Wasted no time finding you.
Sorry. Sorry I did not.

REPAIR

Angels seem likely in this light.
The miracle that you suppose
Truth's only casualty is flight.

Prone on a twin-tub lid, you rose,
Eyes shut, and hovered in the air
The time it takes to salt potatoes.

And there was nothing to repair
When, no one home to catch or scold,
This got repeated on the stair.

Again intensify the cold,
Stare at the god till all is bright,
And let the miracle take hold.

COMPANIONS

We held buttercups to our chins,
Lathered our hands with bright green bars of Fairy.
Now we are both gone,
Disappeared into lives where there's no telling.
I never miss you.
One day, though,
One sunny afternoon with you I would call back.
Will you remember it?
We lay, we squatted
In a white tent
Playing a game it seemed we'd always known.
(I loved it, loved
The buttery flatness of your skin.)
Do you remember,
My oldest, always-young companion,
Lost the moment
We looked at each other
As we'd not looked before?

MY BROTHER S

The sticking click of a piano key,
My belt's S-clip: they stowed my brother's name.
He'd whistle-hiss himself impatiently
Through his teeth (his headstone teeth). His essence. *Him.*

The ribbed sand was a bed of esses too.
That holiday I fished continually –
My catch frustration, which was nothing new –
My brother said to give up on the sea

And took me inland, to fish permitless
The fresh waters. We couldn't find them. Then
It started to come on, as rain's faint hiss
Turned to a deluge – my young rage again.

While my brother laughed and sang laughingly
Through his teeth (his starry teeth). His essence. *He.*

MICROSCOPE

My Christmas present was a microscope,
A box of slides of what God only knew.
I tended them, small beekeeper, in hope
That here was life unfantasised and true.

The humdrum Science soon gave way to Art:
Those psychedelic smears, my first Kandinskys,
Stirred feelings in my loins and then my heart.
It riddled me. I wanted its disease.

My mum, though, saw a boy turned question-mark.
Olivier's Heathcliff, Clark Gable's Rhett
Were her idea of Man, formed in the dark.
I drew strange glances from the kitchenette.

I rolled the focus wheel until she gathered
The thing I was intent on filtering out
Included her. And thus a boy unfathered
At once blinded himself and sowed a doubt.

BOARD GAME

We played and played the Royal Game of Ur,
Four brothers not at one another's throats
One Christmas morning. All the time it took
To stack small victories up, our world shook.

The board, a relic from a royal tomb,
Brought something more familiar home, but what?
What kept us on our knees? ('Funny,' said Aunt,
'How it's the simple present that they want.')

I think it was the dark past fixed us there
With cracked skull, smashed column, blood-sticky hair.

CREATURES

Not to go downstairs
Where daylight has no secrets left,
But to curl up with basilisks of sleep
(You know them, and they know
You inside out; they will not mother you).

Where are they now? And what is this
Vertiginous plain, so like a chequerboard?
Perhaps it's the magnetic one you held
Above your face in bed when still a boy,
Nightmare defying.

Such limbs as pleading reach to you
Would pull you under. Wake instead
And go with slippered feet downstairs,
Uncoupled from sleep's creatures:
Dream-fervid, you might tempt them into day.

GIRL IN A PHOTO

1

Flowers, feathers, the lamp's heated dust
Yellowing in my hand recall
Years spent in awe of others' lust.

So foolish, now, this holding back
Among the swirling-patterned mauves
Of a photograph's lost bric-a-brac.

Behind the smudged settee, at ease,
A smiling long-haired girl suggests
That sex existed, and could please.

Her warmth was for an older man
Who's now ridiculously young.
I learned desire catch-as-catch-can

From her and others as remote
Until one poor girl forced her tongue
Into my mouth, and held my throat.

2

Always it seems
That life's in tune
With *who we were*
Or *how it was.*
Discordant notes
Sound only now –
At least, grate most
Through plotless days,
No end foreknown.

A barefoot girl
Whose smile close up
Brought someone back
From years ago:
Her likeness joins
That day to this,
Will leave, I know,
Two girls distinct,
But one preferred.

3
'A woman, not a girl.'
I hear your bristling complaint
And, nonchalant, turn a dead leaf
Underside up to mark the page instead.
I wouldn't want you falling to the floor
Again from books of mine.
What's to say?
I liked the life you brought
Into a house that death had curtained round.

You were a royal pain,
Impossible to contradict. You said
Only a man who'd shaved could grow a beard;
Keeping one cat was cruelty (you had two).
A hundred times I've shrivelled up,
Meeting your like. Alive,
You do not constitute a ghost –
And so I'll call you that,
Dear ghost, dear girl, my dear.

BLINDS

Was my mum's mind away? How could she part
With something so comforting in our lives
For such cold clacking knives
That sliced the sky, tore red cloth from my heart?

Science in place of warmth! New-fashioned blinds
Twitched open by a noose-cord this way, that,
Where they hung not-quite-flat:
The mechanism of unlovely minds.

I think of graceful birds whose printed flight
Was always toward a broad enfolded moon;
Wild flowers in (surely) June
Wide open, only darkening at night …

'Are the curtains drawn?' *Then*, night spelled an act
In need of arms at full unhindered stretch,
Not narrowing their reach
As if to minister to one with tact.

STREET TUNE

The streets were clean, not mean,
In the new town where we grew.
Close, crescent, orchard, avenue:
What tied them all together, like a ribbon?
The ice-cream van,
The ice-cream van that played
A tune to call us out
To limp along the kerb, beside the thorns,
Or press together on a broad bright path.
Like a thief
That tune broke in
Just when, it seemed, ice cream had slipped from mind.
The tune changed over time,
Like us, like our crazes,
But in my head it's now
Greensleeves, Greensleeves alone.
Greensleeves is all my joy.

VIEW-MASTER

An old world's bravely new here, in a box
That comes alive when tilted to the light.
Reel One – NIAGARA FALLS – Canadian side
Slots into place, over the frayed, off-white,

Trick-optic screen. Blinding technology
Gone vintage, like this Ford assembly line
Or still-going 'Spanish aerocar' suspended
Above Niagara Whirlpool; plastic shrine

Offering outmoded visions of the future.
Except, among the power plants, the skyway,
The four-lane steel-arch bridge to New York State,
Comes round one single, slight anomaly –

A girl in blouse and pinafore, walking where
Cherry trees bloom. May no harm come to her.

VISIT HOME

Odds and ends. Ours went in
A Quality Street tin
We kept in the long press.
A sealed togetherness
Of incompatibles:
Loose thread, out-of-date pills
Were one under tin lid.
Our time together's ended
As flesh has gone its ways,
But housed here, unstitched of days.

NEW PENCE

2ps in her camel coat,
A mint, a whirl of liquorice.
Tobacco from a half-smoked fag
Golden, clinging, shaken loose.
A white glove, or the pair balled-up.
2ps in her camel coat.
Chips on a Tuesday, bingo night;
Licking the fingers' vinegar.
2ps in her camel coat,
Fluff caught in a kirby grip.
'Have you been stealing money, son?'
A mint, a whirl of liquorice.

GOODBYE

The door opens and closes.
A freckled girl stands on the step.
She makes me think of raspberry.
She makes me think of blackcurrant.
I am four – thereabouts –
And my red trike has stopped
At the corner of Baillie Drive.
I mustn't ever cross the road.
Across the road a freckled girl
Stands on the step and waves goodbye
Without waving.

NETTIE IN THE 70S

Aunt kept her Luger in a box
And didn't turn it on the vandals
Whose blades unpicked the walls' new paint
On every landing. As she passed,
They moved aside – 'like gents,' she said.

Those tenements at Thornliebank
Stood like sea-devils in the mist.
Inside was warm. Inside was Aunt,
A three-tiered cake stand, Battenberg
And other fancies that we had.

The *Deutsche Grammophon* LPs
Held glamour of her Berlin days
At the Ministry. Now she filed
The claims of 'idle, feckless men'
– Whose ranks were growing.

FIELDHEAD DRIVE

I want to live on Fieldhead Drive,
That's where the tall nettles thrive,
Not between cracks, but in my head,
Alongside two of my loved dead.

Its tenements are not the worst,
Whatever grievances are nursed.
I loved and feared their chimney stacks,
Round pointless windows, and the backs.

Number eleven, if you please.
Turn right at the top. On her knees,
A woman scrubs the landing clean.
She is the landing-scrubbing queen.

I bow to her and get a whiff
Of Ajax. This is the life! If
Life it is, my clinging on
To wisps of shades. Till they are gone.

AUNT PAT

I see you in a yellow light
Buttering the mashed potato.
You know you're not really my aunt,
And it's too soon to go

On about all that happened there
In the vivid house by the lane.
That house you kept kept you, a wild
Joy woven with the pain.

'Get up the stairs you little bugger,'
You said, chasing me from the room,
Your fine brow of a sashed beauty,
That one time, packed with doom.

A comic 'Que sera, sera'
Can bring you back, as song will do.
But no sharp turn at Paton's mill
Brings me to you.

UNCLE JOHN

After a long day at the surgery
Doling out prescriptions and charisma,
My golfer uncle, urged on by my mother,
Took me out with the clubs, but not to play –

Mercifully for me there was no ball,
My whole problem being I couldn't connect
Cleanly with one. My uncle, to instruct,
Mixed pipe smoke with his words, a warm blue pall.

I heard him but more clearly heard the trees
That lined the disused railway, the old mill.
Everything slowed to a standstill. I stood still,
A supplicant with slightly bended knees.

'What were you aiming at?' 'Nothing, nowhere.'
You mean, I thought, *there is a point to this?*
Though inside he praised my swing to the skies,
We both knew I'd be hitting empty air.

SONS

They're gone from there;
Not even the odd weekend sees them back –
The roving sons
Who slammed each other's heads once in the grass
Until the kitchen light was all there was.

Gone. Then going through a drawer
That stuck at first, lined with old wallpaper,
I joined them, in a glare of unsunned skin,
Stoning the passing cars for recreation.

PATON'S MILL

This mill,
Recently the world's
Oldest machine factory,
Once stood
In one boy's Eden,
An emblem of fear
At the end of the garden,
Its tower
Pointing accusingly
To heaven – at least,
The leaden sky over Johnstone.

Whether you are a lover
Of all things green
Or a worshipper of the machine,
It matters that this mill –
So fine,
So fearful,
Burnt
Almost to the ground –
Now cannot stand
Intact through other days,
In other Edens.

WHITE SHOE

I have my memories, as others do.
Mine make me me, yours make you you.
Why again this, so strong and true –
Putting white polish on a shoe?
White cream shoe polish, one white shoe
That my left hand's holding onto.

It all comes effortlessly into view.
The sky is summer-childhood blue.
One brother's there, my mother too.
The polish oozes like white glue
Over a kind of sandshoe
Pure white already: it is brand-new.

I remember what, I remember who.
The company I was used to.
Was it the colours let all through?
The white so white, the blue so blue.
Or smells of polish, a new shoe?
I'll never know – and hope that's true.

ONE

Just for that one moment,
It seemed as if nothing moved
And all moved. I leant
Back into the oak's trunk,
Looked up at the green crown –
Not resting, unresisting –
And knew no fear or hate,
Just for that one moment.

GOING HOME

I'm going to the black hill,
The street of chimes,
The root of the lopped tree.

To the place of the press,
The immersion,
The torn-down utility,

I'm going to bring my good dream.

AGE

'Age doesn't come alone,'
My brother writes, before his op.
Can it be true? The two of us,
Who fought like sparrows in the gutter,
Will be old like the old women
Met at the shops, in plastic headscarves,
Who muttered as we looked away:
'It's one thing after another'?
Each took an age to go, trundling
Her trolley, well zipped up, behind.

Get yourself out of there, brother.
There's good stuff left I'll fight you for.

THE ROOM

She came to die at last
Because our back room was
Without basins, gauze,
Flighty or harassed
Women pushing past.

In parcel-papered drawers
She put away her things:
A rosary, no rings,
Nothing intimately hers,
Who'd seen Victoria, wars.

I walked upstairs afraid
She'd hear me and call out,
Ask me to be devout
In the bedroom where I played.
Her whole death she stayed.

MISSED THE MOMENT

At ninety-four, my gran wore one patched skirt,
Keeping her good clothes for another day,
Which never came. There was the time at school,
In the lunch queue, when Paul McCafferty,
Shivering with pleasure at the thought of chips,
Said: 'Actually, this is the best bit:
Not eating them, *thinking* about eating them' –
Truth we didn't know we knew till he said it.
And now, today, dressed in my near-worst clothes,
Growing thin on just the thought of breakfast,
I feel, as Voznesensky did, intense
Nostalgia for the present. Then what's missed?
A moment's absorption as the mask slips
And we taste love on chapped, chip-salty lips.

THE PREFECT

On hot days the queue would snake
Inside the toilet, right out the door,
Starting at the drinking fountain –
That V-shaped sink with stubby water-spout –
As young boys who'd run their chests sore
Aped and bobbed but kept in line
Obedient to the prefect
Who sat by the sink in a broken chair
Gleefully metering the water
By counting to ten, now slowly, now quickly,
So that – as we all could see –
The youngest got least, his pals their fill.

Inside I swelled
With rage that overflowed outside:
To a small crowd that listened meekly
I promised that, when my time came,
Every boy would be allotted
The exact-same amount of water: enough
To slake his thirst.

A summer later, I sat,
A prefect (not a bad one),
Fed up with the noise, the stench of piss,
And counted over a small boy's head
'Onetwothreefourfivesixseveneight …'
And didn't even get to ten
Before recalling my younger thirst
For justice in that very place.

No big deal, right?

Why is it, then, when I catch my eye
In that remembered piss-wall mirror
I see a proffered reed
With, at its tip, a sponge soaked in vinegar?

SWEET CHEAT GONE

It's ages ago now
I won a prize unfairly
In Mrs Robinson's living room.
Looking back, I see
Mrs Robinson knew
Fine well what I was doing –
Wrinkling my nose to twitch
The blindfold up a bit.
I pinned that donkey's tail
A little too precisely,
Mrs Robinson, didn't I?

God knows why it's back again,
That lost illicit love
Of victory and liquorice
At any cost, my shame
Lifting the blindfold a little
In Mrs Robinson's living room.

THE CARDS

Game after game of 'ledgy stauner'
In the playground: try as I might,
I couldn't get my cards to stand upright
On any ledge. (I never had the honour
Of being good at spitting, whistling, or playing
Ledgy stauner.) The cards were mugshots
Of English league players – a good few Scots
Among them (I'm only saying);
Wrapped with the cards, a wad of bubble gum,
So oldstyle young men, longhaired or balding –
Tall, gap-toothed strikers; wizards of the wing –
Could shed their bad-boy air and come
Out reeking of strawberry. We held them holy
And by their edges, poring over
Every feature of man and card before
They hit the dirt. Ledgy stauner!
                               The lowly
Were our gods. And though we were taught good deeds
Combined with faith would get us into heaven,
I had my own vision of virtue then:
The pristine whiteness of Don Revie's Leeds.

ANOTHER TIME

Just as my brother took me down
The lighthouse steps and we stood under
Those beams more pointed than I'd thought,
I knew he was reliving then
Another time, when the same wonder
Was even brighter in his eyes.

That was all right, but what was wrong
Was thinking of the times I'd stood
Beside another, pointing to
Some sight that blinded me to her
And a truth Corsewall Lighthouse told:
Not hell but time is other people.

BROKEN

We keep these broken things –
The listing, buckled clothes-horse,
More asinine than equine;
The pedal-less pedal-bin –
In part because we're broken too,
Or else captivated. Well,
What else has childhood to pore over
But every square inch of interior,
Whatever's cracked or warped or peeling,
And the house furniture become the mind's?
Love doesn't struggle to remember
When all was liable to hold.
How things were in the beginning
And how things came to be –
That's the breaking story.
And so we keep this knackered crap
Not to remind us, but because
We've grown to love – at least, got used to –
The fissures, scrapes, exposed workings
Of the living-with-us inanimates
That yet resemble old war horses
Heroically indifferent to their fates.

AGAIN!

The pew-gap was a teller's till
To pass the hymn book through
In lieu of cash. Love one another?
'Next, please.' I tapped my pen.

The disciplined communion queue,
Just like the bank's on Friday,
Induced a rage I had to smother
Until the last 'Amen'.

The fresh air swept it all away.
Hands held, I hung and swung
Between my brother and my mother
Again, again, again!

RHYMED

My life rhymed then: the kitchenette
Beyond the television set;
Tools needing brawn, agility,
Unused in the utility;
The never-materialising fall
Between the landing and the hall;
Our names, the years, graffitied there
Beneath the blooming wallpaper.
The known contour of each slab-crack
Muddied a finger out the back,
While inside, cracks along the ceiling
Told that the patient wasn't healing.
As a matter of fact, all was cracked;
Rhyme kept the whole shebang intact
And does still. In the patient's brain,
No diminution of the pain.

GODMOTHER

She died today, I'm sure of it
– My Godmother, immortalised
In this photo in which she holds me
Still for the priest's blurred, blessing hand:
And that, mere days after my birth,
Was the closest that we two got …
Though some years on, I'm clambering in
To the back of her oddbod car,
And she drives me to school at night
Where I play at being a wolf cub
And she Akela …

                The priest's hand,
Moving, is the one thing blurred;
All else is as clear as the day
I played with her son Peter's toys,
Imagining I had for mother
This dyed-in-the-wool, dyed-blonde Tory
Who may – who knows? – be changed in death
And, from safari-suited car,
Regard my woes like buffaloes.

Help me to herd them, Akela.

SCHOOL LESSON

I watched Năstase in the dark
And rooted for that charming clown.
The television set on stilts
Glowed on me alone, while Mum
Worked in a stink of chemicals.
Where love was naught, the umpire would
Keep score but couldn't cheer or jeer:
He was an English sort of God.

Strange, that a thing so warm at home
Felt chilling in this different place;
Familiar too.
                    In the big school
I wasn't at yet, in the dark
Of a back room in hot July,
I got, half-got, or didn't get
That in this black void where we are
Clown-charm gets us only so far.

MY WEIRD WAYS

I found myself this morning
Getting dressed in the kitchen where it's warm,
And thought of when my brother walked to school
Sucking and chewing on his balaclava:
Anything for comfort. Not that
There wasn't love, but
The love had been interfered with, by death.
Don't mock me, then.
My hillwalker's socks at the height of summer,
My wide shirt wrapped around me like a cloak
Tell their own story – I've told it myself
Many times. Allow me that. My weird ways
Are clutchings at whatever warmth there was,
However much there is now. Don't mock. Only
Reproach me for the coldness I display.

JOKE

Just my luck. The only joke
I ever could remember had
A punchline that required explaining
To anyone my age. My dad
Had left behind his dad-music,
But not this one. 'There is a song,
I Left My Heart in San Francisco,'
I prefaced. The joke itself, too long,
Involved an angel with a harp
And someone by the name of San Pan.
Of course, it was in San Pan's disco
The harp was left. 'That's not the tune,'
Said a heckler (he was my friend).
I scoffed, but knew he had me beat,
Though others did laugh, in the end.

His dad's record collection was more complete.

GIBB'S THING

The boy who blocked my way from school
Has died a lonely death in Jersey.
A down-and-out, by all accounts,
Or as good as. Now this fine day
Is darkened by the thought of him.

Some are inventive in their hate,
Not Gibb: the standoff at home time
Was Gibb's thing. Just beyond the gate,
The touchline of the rugby pitch,
He'd be there, rain or shine, his face
A mass of freckles with a smile
Radiating gormless menace.
Some words were said, but not many,
Some shoving done, but not much.
This play lasted a while – for weeks –
Till he got bored, or lost his touch.

Home time. And he was in no hurry
To get there; in truth, nor was I.
Gibb, what were you doing in Jersey?
What did you still have to defy?
Tough boy, you know you look so fey
In this light.
                    I'll not block your way.

The Stranger

THE BRIGHT TETHERS

Where does he go now, if not into ditches,
Like the parson unsteady on his bicycle,
This man for whom life ceased to have meaning?
He let it go, the secret, like a great fib
We are glad to be rid of, the greatest secret
No loved one, even, gets to share with us.

He let it go, and himself went, unshaven,
Not as on Sunday mornings, the lie-ins:
This time he had a desperate look on him.
Is he at peace, yet, among nettles?
Who will find him, now he has slackened
The bright tethers that had bound him to his life?

SUSPICION

Though you know me so well,
You still regard me
With suspicion

Watching from a corner of your mind
As I move stealthily
In the sun

Like a cat, like a wildcat
Eyeing you as the enemy
Who share my prison.

We are alike, knowing a love
Of silence and of safety.
You find me asleep at dawn

But retract your claws in a show
Of touching mercy
So that the game between us can carry on.

THE FLAW

This is the hardest part, to tell
Your life's tale, and make yourself visible
To yourself, not Beauty and not Beast,
In a room where visibility's least,
As though accounting for another's crimes.
You work hard at it, shuddering sometimes
As though cold water trickled down your back.
And when hope's at its highest you step back
To admire the work whole, but spot a flaw
You couldn't see close up. The flaw is you,
Following, being you, everywhere:
Cast is the man, and counted every hair.

Which brings me to today, and today's entry.
This is not what I wanted to say.

THE MOON'S THUNDER

'I inhabit a dark world.' Why, I wrote
Those words in better days. Going back to recover,
I see us two still, blowing on a flame
Under the moon's thunder, twin sprigs of fire.

I think I invented the colour green
In that landscape. Probably it was winter.
There's no connection with now except that something
Throws a switch, forcing me to remember.

And again I am a child. In that painting
By Rousseau, I am the negro clown
Dancing, having slept for centuries
The good sleep of the dead and the unborn.

THIS SOLITUDE

The fleshless man, whose wrecked machinery
Careers past houses that are made of glass,
Impresses himself on the scenery
But is nowhere; cannot be said to pass
Those recent mothers cooing over cots,
Whose green flesh sprouted and expressed a need.
All flesh is grass: trimmed, in allotted plots;
Or growing dishevelled; or gone to seed.

Somewhere I am, not here; a certain wood,
A dirt path, not this tenement window's
Long tombstone of light on which the cat sleeps.
The damp blackens the wall and my flesh creeps
And the wind blows. I'm not here, don't hear those
Sounds from the fire invade this solitude.

BORDER COUNTRY

Is that your ideal, then, a people
Hard-bitten, with no trace of compassion?
A place so solidly real your impression
Counts for nothing? At a concealed entrance
A sign – *No private gods* – flashes past.
You laugh, seeing your mistake. The boats dance
In the water alluringly (if you could hear them
They would be chiming). What is the smart cast
Of businessmen and aesthetes doing here,
Playing at having roots? You are one of them.
You think, passing the scrapyard, *This is what we are –*
Wrecks, piled on top of one another,
And a drab grey bird flying over.

The last escape of blue is swallowed up
In cloud pack. Cars put on their lights.
Hands holding steering wheels are guiding kites
As minds drowse through the passing border country.
Savage place! Tam Lin between the trees,
Mother-naked, eyes grey as the sea,
Reminds you of a lawless, Godless code.
You think you hear dinner-gongs in the breeze
As you exit the rasping stony road
For smooth, and silent, surfaces. Not your home;
It never was. Your own home, your own people
Keep getting in the way, spoil your ideal.
You sit scowling, welded to the real.

MY ENEMY

He keeps me in this hovel, serves me drinks.
I secretly admire him, he thinks.
Sham wisdom shining from his owl face,
With crazy logic he presents a case
I can't refute, argues his necessity.
'You'll learn,' he says, 'in time to live with me.'

My enemy trips me up, time after time,
And I never learn. *What was my crime?*
Is a senseless question I don't ask.
He brings me books, and fruit, and a fresh task
Each day. Each day I fail to complete it,
And feel the merciless, sharp edge of his wit.

BLOOD ORANGE

Eating a blood orange, remembering
Not one line of all you wrote
But yourself as a boy sitting
On grass too sharp to pull, you thought:
Exchange for that child's grimace then
This present misunderstanding (fair play
If he asks for his old self back again,
Gets refused, cries bitterly) –
What sort of monster have you made?
A boy gone out of his mind,
Still playing every game you played,
Who's hidden well, whom you'll never find.

THE CENSOR

Don't write. Don't rake up the leaves.
Your poems aren't a sacred script.
What right have you to wound silence?
I'd like to see your body stripped,

Excrement daubed on your cell wall
Before you come in angry and
Shaking your head at human passion.
I'll fight to have these scribblings banned.

Your private life's a public zoo
In which you ape yourself and bluff
A way to your own heart. You suffer?
Your sentence isn't harsh enough.

THE STRANGER

And in the dream (for where else meet
You, my too familiar stranger?)
I caught your scent – not bitter, sweet
With the sweetness that sugars danger.

I had tears for how odd you looked.
And now closing my eyes I see
A staring woman, make-up streaked
Across a face unsettling to me.

It's strange hearing the dead unburden
Themselves in dreams, to feel revive
Old sorrows for them; more so when
Their real life counterparts are alive.

'I'm not saying it didn't hurt or
It went smoothly either. You go
Unwillingly, or not, the fear
In dying lonely is that you'll *know.*'

She smudged her make-up with one hand,
With the other touched me suddenly.
'I can expect you to understand.
Look round me: there's no scenery.

I went like a bride to the dark.'

FIELDS OF WHEAT

I walked through fields of wheat on blue-black nights.
The clear moon soothed me, I was pierced
By the scent of pine;
And the landscape was mine.

Putting my Rousseau harlequins in the frame,
I found I couldn't make my last escape.
History wasn't through
With me yet, I knew.

Sardonic smiles, tears of tenderness.
Like you, I grow older, knowing less;
Again as I was once:
Not harlequin, but dunce.

What's left to me's a field, a broken tree;
In the Last Supper or my next meal,
The hope that solitude
Will be some kind of food.

THE SUM

You wrapped in your lonely coat
This green night breathe in the stars.
What's the sum of all you wrote?
A dog's bark the wind scatters.

TWO FRIENDS

They told their dreams along an avenue
Bright with the sea, and came to a stone square,
A pier house where lobster pots were kept;
Dodged the old-man pub – white dominoes,
Tables scrubbed – and tinkling, chiming jetty.
In the salt air, dreams made sense to them,
And they walked like that an hour, memorably at ease.

One wanted to kill his father's ghost,
One to win back the love of a married woman.

VOICES

Voices, spiders on the stair.
Inside the rooms
A man is talking to his son
About a pigeon.

Walls have become opaque,
Which were glass before.
Sunlight replicates
The swing-park's geometry on one.

How the afternoon sickens!
After the senseless songs,
After the patient, slow
Stirring of food –

To be eaten in silence
Lasting a lifetime now.
The white one's albino.
(The pigeon, the pigeon.)

REVELS

Said Clubfoot to No-foot,
'May I have this dance?'
Grasshoppers on the curtain
In an unseemly trance

Marvelled at these revels.
'Daughter, you look so pale.
Here's bed and some sedative.'
'And here's salt for your tail.'

ENTRY

It's puzzling, the small window.
A lad called Jack could have got in,
Surprised a man and wife abed
And changed their squalor into sin.

Thieves are right to favour roofs.
The slate will hold against their tread.
They work in landscapes of the moon
Where fears are bright and nothing's said.

THE SINGER AND THE SONG

1
She doesn't try to milk applause,
Crouched like that between each song
To drink the water at her feet.
Too modest, you think. You don't like this.

Enter a man, a snake charmer
Relaxed in his skin. Now sway along,
Stupefied in the moment's heat.
You care less for his songs than her.

2
Since *Oranges and Lemons* holds the key
In that 78 you took on Sunday,
You go out on a limb so far you say
That music was your mother more than she.

You scratched it, and it's never been the same.
Perhaps you cried then. Now, no tears, a frown.
But if she'd only not been broken down,
She could have sung the song, escaped your blame.

SONG: BLACK-EYED SUSAN

Black-eyed Susan was my daughter,
Black-eyed Susan was my daughter.
She lived in a caravan
With her lousy boyfriend dealer
And their skinny whippet, Sheila.
Well, I had to end that scene.
Gentlemen, I think you know just what I mean.

Here's the tune, I paid the piper.
Here's the tune, I paid the piper.
There is no end to the week.
I have seen the dance of barflies
Up against a Glasgow sunrise,
And, exhausted on the ground,
The lovers lose the pleasure that they'd found.

Never go to church on Sundays,
Never go to church on Sundays
Just to hear some sweaty priest.
You can count on his devotion
At the bottom of emotion
No matter what you've done,
So go on and lie on beaches in the sun.

HER DRESS

I found a flat stone on the beach
That made me think of you,
And set about it with a rock
And broke that stone in two.
Did you feel it on your rounds,
Or on your barstool sinking down,
Some floozy next to you?
You told me nothing's out of bounds
When I was your sad little clown,
And what you said was true.
So I'll shatter you.

The lights are winking, one by one,
The sea is sighing back.
I'll put the big tarpaulin on
To make the whole lot black.
While there's gas left in the bottle,
Paraphernalia on the sill,
I know you could be back.
I only need that thought to settle,
And even if I don't sleep well
I'm happy in the sack
With no man at my back.

This is the dress I wore the day
You first clapped eyes on me,
And it's the dress I'll wear the day
My father buries me.
If I outlive that devil, I
Will send his smoke up to the sky
And watch him drift from me,
Just like the time you left and I
Thought of you as the window-fly;
Pretended not to see
You wash your hands of me.

NEWCOMERS

Dogs in the lane scent strangers, two at first.
We quickly breed suspicion in their eyes.
Appeasing words or gestures are the worst.

The length of a lane we live like foreign spies.
O few can know themselves to be as cursed
Or intimate with intrigue and disguise.

ALL ELSE

There's always one neglected room
In strange house dreams, where water seeps.
Familiar, quite unlike a womb,

It is the sex you never had,
The novel you insist is in you,
The courage to be wholly mad.

If you'd been left straw-haired and wild,
Your hands not made to seem dead weights
And you a wet, unsmiling child …

Now the asthmatic sleeper's head
Turns to the faintly moving curtain.
All else lies paralysed in bed.

FOR MISS X

1

Yawning from counting colours on an abacus,
Complacent as the circling fish, eye off the ball,
You've just pictured the girl next to you take a piss,
When out it comes: the feared, loved word. And you could crawl.

Of all calamities, the most calamitous:
To call out 'Mum' in class, instead of 'Miss'.

2

Doh, ray, me, fah, soh, lah, te, doh
Directs the twitching of her marking pen,
Alone survives the silence she's commanded
Moments after Mum's said.

3

A ghost's wife,
A ghost herself, nearly,
She glides to bed across the unlit landing
With no one left now to quieten down
Except for the night's dead who speak so queerly.

Isn't this
Right, Miss?

THE STABLE BOY'S SONG

The stable boy sang
To the unstable girl.

They were leading out the ponies
On Dunfanaghy beach,
He swinging his free arm,
She biting her lip.
'When did you turn eleven?'
'Don't know.'
                    'When's your birthday, then?'
'Don't know.'

At that he sang,
'O Coraline,
With the black sewed-on button eyes.'

DIMINISHED

When I lie down it will be bright enough
To make out shapes of bookshelves and their books
And dark to see the light displays of cars.
Now memory makes a vivid last appeal:
My father swatting midges from my hood,
Diminished to a tool-box after death;
A party where I pulled out all the stops
And pouting girls looked largely unconvinced;
Those mushroom-gatherers on that gleaming hill.
I root around for meaning in this heap
(The neighbours call a muffled word or two):
Ready or not, sleep's ambush comes like age,
Obliterating what's not understood,
Or so it seems tonight. Others may lie
And claim they saw it all or had it whole.

I looked for God. I found a barber's pole.

REVELATION

The epileptic girl shouts up
To the woman who disappears
And reappears at intervals
But not to lead the girl inside.
All this is happening without
Intervention of passer-by.

The girl shouts words the kids all want
To shout at mothers too sometimes.
They look wild-eyed at one another,
But nothing happens. She shouts up
Emptily, mechanically, as
The woman moves across the glass.

Next to the new-town terraces,
At a pale scattering of trees,
Come to this place for friendship, love,
One boy is also coming to
The stark and unutterable
Conclusion that God is evil.

MEIN HOSTS

I climbed the stair. The two below
Whispered again. 'Don't go
To too much trouble,' he said.
'It's already trouble,' she said.

ENCOUNTER

She gave the boy with the bad eye holy water
After the bus pulled out of Dungannon station.
She had rosary beads in a loop of her jeans
And 'Tough enough,' she said, 'God willing' and 'Grand, grand';
Finally, 'No, I've no husband.' The bad-eyed boy
Got off at Maguiresbridge without her number.

IT ALL

In memory of Ian Curtis

'This is the room, the start of it all.'

A ward,
A terraced house in Barton Street;
A birth cord,
A kitchen-pulley rope.
Not unattached you came and went
Through a room-partitioned world where one
Barely exists at all, is nothing at all.

Camp-victim sex slaves,
'Joy Division':
Numbers
Branded on their skin.
Not tasteful to appropriate the name
For some post-punk band from Salford.
Then I think:
Training Services Division.
You who, in offices, spoke so civilly
Did you draw on that division you were in,
Substituting 'joy'?

Four boys, flirting with dark aesthetics,
Rehearsed in rooms until they made a sound
That rent the heart in two, rent it with joy.
And with an icy stare, convulsed even,
You gave it all
And tried, and failed, to take back what you gave.

Hypnotically regressed, you said you were
'Just reading … a book about laws …
And going over bits … and keeping notes.'
That Kafka spirit, as cramped in Macclesfield
As his was in Prague,
Craved something that was not in any room:
Not in the bedroom, not in the bathroom,
Not in the living room, not in the kitchen –
Unless it was in the kitchen all along.

THE OPERATION

'Plum's Disease,' the doctor-surgeon said,
Face *über-strikt*. Unfazed, I said:
'That can't be bad, can it? I mean, *Plum's*.
Where did I catch that?
In the conservatory, with a candlestick?'
'It's serious,' the doctor-surgeon said,
Hoisting a rope, in synch with his assistants.
And as the operating table rose
Towards the dreadful sun-hole, I reflected
On plums and suchlike fruit.
'Thin it may be, but a plum-skin's resilient;
Nor is my heart a stone.'
'You're focusing,' the doctor-surgeon said,
'Too much on the part *Plum's*.'
I took his hint. Prone on that wooden disk, though –
How come they towered over me? Were they on stilts? –
Unease was all I felt. 'Hold him down, boys.'
'For pity's sake, leave it inside me, then.'
I clocked his face. A muscle twitched. Reprieve?
'No can do,' he said, and his assistants
Chirruped in chorus.

JOCKEYING

Joker says to Harlequin:
'That top's too tight for you.'
Harlequin says: 'You mean, Sir,
Ill-fitting clothes speak shame,
This sorrow I've outgrown.'
'It's all one to me, kid,
What you think,' says Joker.

'But while we're on the subject,
That hair could do with a cut.'
Harlequin says: 'You'd rather
See clearly my icy stare
Which penetrates your hollows.'
Joker thinks for a minute,
Says: 'Kid, we know you suffer.

The rest of us suffer too.'
Harlequin blinks in the mirror.
'Is *suffering* behind
That colourful cap'n'bells?'
Joker clears his throat, says:
'I see My One Weakness
Romped home today at Ayr.'

LOST

The crystal rose
Turns on its stem,
Twists in no wind,
The crystal rose.

There was a cow
Fell in the canal.
Why that cow fell
I cannot tell you now.

A bright paper moon
I'd have hung aloft
From scented rafters,
A bright paper moon.

Here's to the day
That could not be
When her blood and my blood
Rose up in flood.

WELL

A young man, I sat
In a cathedral,
Telling myself all was well.

But all was not well,
In or out of a cathedral,
Then or after that.

PRAYER

Unknown prisoner,
Imagined on waking,
You offer me no comfort. I pray
That when the daylight
Throws shadows grown homely once more,
You will wear your innocence lightly,
Like a shirt, a clean shirt
Which loving hands left out and smoothed for you.

GREETINGS

How're you?
                    Baffled newcomers
Turn to narrate their state of health
To empty air. I walked here once,
The question raging for reply.
How'm I? How would you say I am?
The man who walked his dog, who walked
Tilted like Lear into the wind,
And would say nothing, only point –

Had a house fire, walks as before
But without his dog. There's a story.
I can discern none in nature.
Better to walk in it, be greeted
For the first mile then not at all;
Walk myself out, go back to find
The grate's still black and my elder
Son can spell 'apple'.
                    Yes, I'm well.

BREAKDOWN

Those sudden houses,
Painted a petrified-blue –
Who lives in them? Men do,
But not alone. You picture one
Mending a fence, a dog
Doubling as his shadow,
Wife in the cool of the kitchen,
Unschooled kids at large.

You met him once
The day your dashboard blinked a warning
Not seen by you before.
You got out, inspected your fear,
Climbed the muck slope as best you could.
He was there by a shed.
With a curt word he sent the kids inside,
Walked slowly over …

Christ, I'm well out of that, you thought,
Flashing your hazard lights in thanks
For the wrong directions, the push
That somehow got you going again
– Home, to your wife, come strolling out
Paint pot in hand, with puzzled look
That you should say so lovingly:
'Magnolia.'

ROGER TO SYD

I praise a man called Roger
Who changed his name to Syd
Then changed it back again.
Madness can't say what it did
For madness is not lucid
Either in Roger or in Syd.

Roger could become Syd,
Syd could not become Roger:
That's the long and short of it.
He was not just some codger
Living in his mum's old house;
But nor was he Roger.

If it takes two to know, then Syd
Knew. Not only Syd,
Roger – before not after Syd
Went mad, and wasn't Syd:
Not the Syd who passed for Syd
When he was Syd.

SELF CONDEMNED

Who was it that I murdered once,
And won't let me forget at night,
Buried beneath my restless eyes?

The parts of whose dismembered corpse
Are eaten by the pasty-faced
Cannibal-criminals of dream.

I'm no murderer, I murmur,
Dry lips parting in the morning
For tea and toast. My last breakfast?

OF THE PLANTS

1
Saxifrage and tormentil,
Tormentil and saxifrage:
One a rock-breaker, one
An astringent for the ill.

2
Take tormentil, derived
From the Latin *tormentum*,
'Which signifies such gripings
As the herb serves to relieve';

This blood root's red dye
Springs from the same tannins
That turn hide into leather,
Make mouths puckery and dry.

3
To Bernadette at Lourdes,
The command: 'Eat of the plants.'
Pyrenean foothill, Alpine peak;
Near springs, and in wet woods:

The many saxifrages.
Each bloom, in opening, turns
From a bell into a star,
As every man and woman is.

DEFEAT THE ROBOT

Say something new
Or say something old in a new way.
Go on, surprise yourself,
Defeat the robot
Who revels in your prime,
Puts all your time to waste.

You can defeat him, not destroy him –
Or if you try,
Be sure the hand you die by
Will be his.
Defeat the robot. Taste
The salt wind at an interstice of time.

REQUEST

And if I am my body,
Shall I rise completely,
Like the sun above a hill,
Untormentedly to shine,
Announcing 'This is morning'?

And if I am my soul,
Shall I stand entranced
By the sea, and send my beams,
Identifiably mine,
To those that forever pass?

Heart, reconcile these two.
Find me some calm between
Unhindered early morning
And cramped last-thing-at-night
To feel you and to feel me.

A COUNTRY SUPPER

As well this charming supper hostess,
Or hell's own hound,
Whose unpredictable stallion
Pounds the ground.

What love is made could start a fire
On Hampstead Heath.
The cork walls dampen down the sound
Of chattering teeth.

Remembering the scars acquired
Without a fight
But at their hands, I sit and smoke
Near half the night …

In Libya, the liberal king
Had floors to tile,
And when the colonel ousted him
We left in style.

I've seen the world, enough of it.
I've cottoned on,
With fingers worked, not to the bone,
Till the feeling's gone.

Even at the top, they're on the up;
We're on our uppers.
In the shires, what a shower
Of country suppers.

THE JACKAL

He's gone through life in terror of the jackal,
But the jackal had its eyes fixed on another.
It's true he was a piece of ravaged meat
In those years holed up in a tenement:
Some nights a snout would sniff around his face.
But the half-meant obeisance he made
He made when he was safely in the clear.
The jackal had its eyes fixed on another,
And one he least expected. So it goes.
The tips that he could give to ward it off
Are only gratitude he was passed over.

FIASCO

I spent Christmas alone;
No, not alone,
My companion
A one-eyed cat called Fiasco.

Being clueless about wine
And the exchange rate of the guilder,
I washed down the roast chicken
With a bottle of dirt-cheap plonk.

In the line of vision
Of that cat's enlarged eye,
I watched Jimmy Stewart
Say 'Thataboy Clarence' – till tears fell.

Hugging the toilet bowl
As I puked up my guts
(The wine, it must have been):
Was that when I felt most alone?

No, there have been worse days and nights
Resistant to anecdote, none
Graced by that matchless cat.
Fiasco!

TREES

Until I walked the lane
And saw the trees – not equally, but all –
Twist in the wind,
I thought I understood my life.

MOST LIVES

Most lives go unremarked, but not unfelt.
Consider this as you pour scorn on all
Trite (if true) sentiment flatly expressed.
The crombie coat that's hanging in the hall
Still has more presence than the man who filled it
To one become a connoisseur of coats.
Pass remark on the wetness of a handshake,
If you must. Don't forget: some mother dotes
On the man himself.   You remember one,
Long before you knew her, at an awkward age,
Sitting down, pen in hand, her crisp diary
Cracked open at the dated, daunting page,
Until words came (they stand for all of those
Ever scorned by you): 'In the morning, rose.'

And After All

THE TEMPLE MONSTER
In memory of Martin Temple

Village of Sorrow

I walk the steep road
Into the blue trees.
The river, curved like a horn,
Blows beside me.
Balfron. Hidden
Eyes drop their salt,
As the ancient, disposed
Body of Fergus
Is trundled along Crow Road.

A Horror Story

It happened in a horror story.
She flashed a look at me I recognised
As your mad look. Thunder literally
Breaking up the sky,
I could go to my grave like this, I thought.
As I was about to die,
I heard a voice downstairs say, 'Breakfast's out.'

Her dream was of a lizard in a love-flower.
Determined to see the day for myself,
I stepped out in a benign April shower.
I was better there,
Not preoccupied with thoughts of your death.
Screaming blue murder,
You folded the knife back into its sheath.

My deafness helps me to recall your voice.
You are up there, somewhere: show yourself.
Could this be one more ending of your choice?
O man amidst the boys,
A girl's mad look brought you back from heaven.
You make no noise.
The weather breaks. The sky's shining like a screen.

Postscript

He went missing, but turned up at my door
Angry, demanding to be fed. I looked
Behind, as though a stranger might overhear,
Or to hesitate, and nearly puked
Seeing a broad blood stain on his coat.
'I'm not good at this,' I said, 'harbouring …'
But he choked the last two words in my throat,
Let go and laughed. 'I never was missing.
So you got it wrong, everything you wrote.
Why won't you listen?' He picked up the phone.
'You're like this mouthpiece: I speak into you
But you don't hear. Or the phone's me – the telling bone,
Catweazle called it. I don't amuse you.'
'You do. You did. You died for nothing.'
He looked me up and down. 'That's what you say.
What was it, you think? An obscure, private hurt
– Or words to that effect? Not exactly.
Don't waste your time raking through the dirt.
The truth is, I was showing you the way.
You always wanted death and now you have it.
I am the suicide you contemplate
But never quite manage. Isn't that right?'
He looked me up and down again, not with hate.
'I extend the cold hand of friendship
To one who is living from one that's dead.'
'We're very alike, I think.' He curled his lip,
Smiled his smile. 'I never noticed,' he said.

From All the Words

From all the words you've spoken
Select one. Select the least word
You mumbled once, your voice broken,
That went unheard.

Break the silence of death
To speak that word aloud.
I swear before you draw breath
I'll have knelt, and bowed.

ANNIVERSARIES

1
We can't decide
Which day it was
You left for good.
We call a truce,
Get in the car
And drive, just drive.

2
Mind in its groove,
In its rut
Remembers a day
Crouched in the sunflowers
And the lake after,
The dogs uneasy.

YOUR PLACE

There are places that haunt the conscious mind,
As this one haunts yours. A small wind
Carries the scent of pine through the fence,
And darkness makes the visible immense
Where it's glimpsed through space. You walked here years ago,
Left charred beds in the grass, prints in the snow;
Scowled at the best of times. Impressed, you stare
At Poet's Peak and the paths everywhere
And notice the difference in the grass,
Matted like hair where so many feet must pass.
Your old haunt, not specific to you,
Occurs in other stories. This was always true,
But grows more noticeable with age:
Yours, the place's. The water turns a page
That you might wish to linger over later;
The paths have been strengthened and made straighter;
Only you have not changed. There are places
Written down, whose names tell you nothing, faces
Glimpsed in the dark of the unconscious mind,
Which not even memory can look behind.

THE CLEAR NOTE

An ordinary meal, with red wine
And clumsy grip muffling the clear note:
Easy to mistake this for a sign,
Imagine hands around one's throat.

The mind's teased in this crude mass
By the delicate patterns on the crystal.
A shriek might shatter the perfect glass,
Blood and wine disgrace the table.

DATES

I date my poems
As you'll date my death:
On completion.
Though in reality
Things happened long before.

MORE TO A MAN

There must be more to a man
Than books about the weather.
He must contain more
Than can be kept in a hamper.

If the damp smell of the loft
Does not wither him,
The wood warp in the ladder,
Steel buckle beneath him,

What is left must stand
Like ripe wheat in the wind –
Or fall, and his memory fail,
And time run out like sand.

IN THE FOREST

1

We heard thunder in the west:
An ancient symbol was sinking down.
We were young then, in the forest.

Didn't we invent the colour green?
Soft crumbling crutches in the sky,
Telegraph poles flecked the scene.

We hated pylons, their slow buzz.
Insects we could sympathise with,
And the moon's scorpion claw was over us.

We invented everything, the dragon trees,
The mushrooms like sea horses in the fields,
And a real horse in one field, a gypsy's.

2

Branches stand for desire.
You drag them through a clearing.
You make the night-fire.

You find me in your Spain.
You make the night-fire.
You make my dead walk again.

ZENNOR

And about Zennor, and my drunken friend, not the one
With bicarb, but the thread dangling from a loose
Button. I like your blue jacket, da, but all the same
The salt etc. breath is a good device for burning
One nightingale in particular. Oh nightingale in the flame.
Think of it, and it never ends, not properly,
Except that Zennor still stands in a high wind
And foxglove bells still can make me shiver.
And the mermaid in the church, I mean both halves of her –
Blue is her colour, but forgive me the purple
Foxglove. Forgive me always the lovely weeds and
Sense of ragged edges. It is not death now the icon,
But real blood forever alive in the last place.

JET

Your jet of blood that always.
Your jet of blood that only.
Your fill of blood that day.

I search foreheads for roots
To find the loved landscape.
The blood-pearls spangle your face.

Her blue becomes my blue,
And music turned by a handle
Enters the place it makes.

FACTORY ROOFS

I knew something, as the swing rose and fell.
I knew: Death can be present in a spirit-level.
I knew there was a whole other world
Beyond the wire.

Tumble down, tumble down, all of us
In fields nettle-infested, fields dandelion-clocked.

AFTER ALL

And after all, the mantelpiece remains,
A roped porthole mirror keeps out the sea.
O still-unsmashed, bright-polished window-panes!
No one can think straight. Only dogs are free.

INCIDENT

This other, this
Intruder, say,
Slept in my place

On pillows he'd
'Had from childhood'.
A certain fake.

How could I rob
Him like a corpse?
Was all my thought.

My mind was cracked.
I leapt out like
Jack from his box.

No suicide
Had met his death
With sweeter breath.

COOKIES

1

You kiss me with an open mouth;
I have no breath to give.
No fortune cookie from my past
Has taught me how to live.

2

Breakfast seems a pleasant meal
When two sit down to talk.
The grass will grow beneath your feet;
You won't know how to walk.

3

The mountains are all hung with lights
Along the frozen coast.
I never understood till now
A man is his own ghost.

AN END

When all I've said and done
Joins all unsaid, undone,
And I consent to lie
And break the butterfly –
That will be when my dirt
Is shaken out the mat;
An end to all the hurt,
An end to all of that:
One coin of Adam's curse
Back in my mother's purse.

AT THE DOOR

I know the secret of the door
Dividing *after* from *before*.
I know who waits there, with black band
To make the children understand.

You know it too. You used to do.
You used to fold my hands in two
And clasp them tight. I pray you find
Him hidden, waiting to be kind.

THE HOUR

How will you fare
In the hour
Of destruction
As the handholds
And the footholds
Slide? Rest assured
It is coming,
And with a warning:
A sudden pain
Behind an eye.

You had your hour
Once before?
But then
You were so guiltless,
So helpless –
Really a jellyfish –
It will be as new.
Nothing grants you
Instruction
For the hour that's here.

IN THE GAP

Who stands in the gap at the door,
Staring down at me as I sleep?
I think it is my cousin John
Back from the pub to play a trick.
'It's all right, you can come out now.'
John doesn't budge, if it is John.

Who stands in the gap at the door,
Staring down at me as I sleep,
As if nothing could be more real?
Is it my old school friend, Tony,
To take revenge for the thrown glass
That last New Year? 'Well, come on then.'

Who stands in the gap at the door,
More menacing than friend or cousin,
Tall, moving like a shaken stick?
I should have known it: Death himself,
Staring down at me as I sleep,
Standing his ground. He knows I'll keep.

CROW

In my chimney
There is a crow.
Do what I will, I cannot make
The crow go.

Hearing him in
So small a space,
I feel my shoulders cramp then itch
To leave this place.

I'll never leave.
He will not go.
My sorrow is, I cannot grieve
For less than crow.

PLEASE NOTE

It goes like this:
The ache you have now you will have thirty years from now;
Whatever you forgave you'll be called on to forgive again
Times without number – and don't count on you being forgiven.
If you can't stand this heat, by all means open a window
And leap from that. The world, assuredly, will remember you
As one who leapt.

CAGED

You don't know what to think or who you are.
I want to die, caged Sybil told the boys.
You'd like to but you never went that far.

To *all that* there can be no *au revoir*.
The act of cowardice requires poise.
You don't know what to think or who you are.

Designs for living – more and more they jar;
Vague plans to starve in attics cleared of toys.
You'd like to but you never went that far.

A monkey can be found at a bazaar,
Cymbals at the ready, making no noise.
You don't know what to think or who you are.

If only you had some convincing scar
To point to, and say: 'See where it destroys.'
You'd like to but you never went that far.

Inertia such as yours could dwarf a star.
And even in the face of simple joys
You don't know what to think or who you are;
You'd like to but you never went that far.

T.A. GOLDEN

Down below my window,
The T.A. Golden store
Looks faded as the bunting.
It isn't golden, has nothing to store.

But Time is the deceiver.
In a sudden close-up,
Veined hands turn from the till,
Smooth out the cloth. T.A. Golden looks up.

THE GLASS OF WATER

The glass of water that I took upstairs
To ward off dehydration in the night
Is still there (undrunk on the banister
Where I left it), like a reproach. What else
That I meant to keep close has been put out
To meet the gaze of any passing ghost?

SONG: OUT OF THE STORM

When the storm hit the bay
At the end of the day
We got up from our beds to look.
At the crash of a wave
That was dark as the grave,
All the walls and our bodies shook.

So we sat in the night
Till the next flash of light
Showed a form we had seen before:
It was torn, it was whole,
It was blacker than coal
And white as it stood in the door.

'Never once did I stray,
Never fell by the way.
Though you thought me in this dear green place,
I have sat by your side,
I have walked as your guide,
Like the stars, at an even pace.'

So the form spoke and then
Joined the darkness again
But we knew on the stroke it was gone
That the stillness we kept
When as babies we slept
Would be ours in the clearest dawn.

TEACHER

The man who taught pathetic fallacy
With too much relish, so I thought,
('No cloud or leaf or stone can feel a thing')
Drank himself senseless while his wife
Cared for their son despite ill health,
The son who likes a drink now too, I'm told …
Sir, we never saw eye to eye,
And now you're gone I'm moved to say
That clouds and leaves and stones are weeping.

YEAR-END

Now that the market sellers have
Set up their stalls in frost, and kids
Raid barrels where the crabs are kept,
And bunting is put up again,
Will I consign my year-end dirge
To the wind, an untied balloon,
And pay the Harvest King his fee,
Which is to see another year
In the place where the laughter's long
In coming, and the men cut down
The girl who couldn't hack it all?

The wind may take it where it will.

I'll walk, head down, and cross the road,
Inspect the dust that lies so thick,
To see a pattern where none is.

M

THE STORY

1

I knew her by her fruits,
The blackcurrant and raspberry;
Felt my own shoots and roots
Stirring, spreading inside me.

She slipped her death-mask on.
I quickly pretended
To convulse in premonition
Of how the story ended.

In the turning key,
In the cistern's whine,
Hear her, skeleton-monkey
Chanting in your spine.

2

I thought I sensed her standing in the rain.
Should I get up and close the blinds again?
'If that's how she intends to trick me,' I said,
'I'll play it cool, lie flat, pretend to be dead.'
I said Hail Marys, I tried counting rain,
I watched dawn breach the sky with its red stain.
'I'll bring her to heel first, and then to bed.
How clever I am, even asleep,' I said.

But then a different voice. 'You spoke, my dear,
Too harshly to my defective ear.'
There lay, in the space where she should have lain,
A skeleton-monkey dripping with black rain.
I woke at that, half-paralysed with fear.
Was this the effect my words had on her?
I lost count of the syllables of rain
And hailstones pressed like thorns into the pane.

SPOKE-WHEELS

Spoke-wheels, can't you forget?
My memory hasn't rusted yet.
It's sunshine on the coverlet.

She draws back, reveals one breast.
In my own home I am her guest.
You, yes you, ah, this is the best.

What's hidden's not a dark smile
But the crisp new pages of my file.
The bastard's me. Put me on trial.

Evil is as evil does.
It's love's flies we hear buzz.
Love was the murderer of us.

Memory's not rusted yet.
It's sunshine on the coverlet.
Spoke-wheels, can't you forget?

CONJURE YOU

Is there a letter that could conjure you?
Or what metamorphosis must I go through?
In whose company would I find you?

Tie up the black parcels with string
And go to their funeral-wedding.
Strip your body, your world, of meaning.

Nothing ever amazes
There, where heaven's explained to us.
It's you, your edge, I've wanted always.

HAND ME DOWN

Not just standing there, lonely, vacant,
I was handed down my grey greatcoat –
Its buttonholes' dark eyes –
In the place where the cracked cornice was.

Some river with a beautiful name
Flowed through walls to where sleep lay.
My life gagged on a crust:
It wanted its own first world kept.

Memory is like firewater there.
So much I longed for Indian Summer,
To know what one was.
It was what women had, in eyes.

NIGHT AND DAY

Difficult, when you find
The crone you steal a look at,
Who lives disgustingly on the hill,
Turns up as Queen of Hearts
In your dream.

And painful, in the dream,
When suddenly at the wood's edge
You feel an old euphoria
That can't be shared, and say
'Something not right here.'

Imposing guests
Excuse our lack of joy.
In daylit rooms
We wonder what to do with them;
What they have to do with us.

PROMENADE

Here, walking on the promenade,
Life's peaceful, possibly corrupt.
No girl doing cartwheels on the beach
Or old man jabbering at his dog
Distracts your thought. But bafflement
Returns with something you once knew:
A world confused, not limitless,
Bold-lined, bright-coloured – childhood –
Where Cartwheel Girl distracted you.

SISTERS

These sisters,
Co-conspirators
In liquid motherhood,
Inspire distress
But no caress.
That's understood.

They will go far
To seem a star
To landlocked men
Whose upward gaze
Once drew their praise
And might again.

O sisters, what
Untimely knot
Have you tied now
To make the world
So small and curled,
Hung from a bough?

ALISON BELL

Alison Bell walks her dog through the streets of her town.
She wears a red coat with a lining as soft as swan's down.

At school she attracted both sexes, revered for a look
Peculiar to then but today just her beauty's her hook.

Born under Cancer with Mariner IV over Mars,
Her great loves were Soviet gymnasts and old Citroën cars.

In dreams she gets on with her dad before waking too soon
Like Tatum with Ryan O'Neal in the film *Paper Moon*.

Alison, Alison, Alison, Alison Bell.
Alison, Alison, Alison, Alison Bell.

FIGMENT

The undertaker shuffled
(He'd heard so many sighs)
As over my dead body
You cast your laughing eyes.

A WALK IN THE WOODS

No, let's *not* go for a walk, Miss.
Couldn't we put off for a bit
Our education in the woods?
Leave it at daisies, dandelions,
Just as they are? Why strip them back
To petal, sepal, stigma, stamen –
Terms you yourself checked in a book
Moments ago?
            On this May day,
I sense it's less for us than you
We're buttoning up our green blazers;
Less work, more longing to recapture
Walks with a man who, days from now,
Will change you from a Hunter to
A Thoroughgood.
              Let's not go, Miss.
We'll not swap yellow light for daylight
Just yet. It could be dangerous.

THE RETURN

Hope sticking in my throat like bread,
I said my piece. The weird sisters –
They seemed weird, and they looked alike –
Maintained a pert poise on the stairs.

The middle one explained: 'We're new here,
Have been … installed since you last came.
We've no news of the ones who left,
But this: we share the family name.'

I watched her watching me and how
I drank her words. The other two
Leant supportive hands on her hands.
Which, if any, or all of you?

I thought, and blushed to think they heard.
'Naturally, you are welcome here,'
The middle one went on, 'though do
Send word first. And not every year.'

I let myself out – I still could –
And felt a secret joy on seeing
The darkened stone, the bright windows
And the weird sisters disagreeing.

THE RING OF TRUTH

1
I'd met the born-again,
Those wounded in childhood,
With shining faces all.
She was different from them,
Steadier in her gaze,
And even just her name
Had the ring of truth.

2
Was she a Muse to God?
She told me she was leaving
To keep house in some
English parish or other.
I wonder do her eyes
Reflect a gleaming kitchen,
Or has she left that place?

3
Has she left that place,
As I've left many places,
To stand at a black railing,
Locked out, in a drift of rain?
I like to think she stayed
For the worthy still to see
Her determined smile.

NOT TO BE

I saw you through the grille.
You had your nose in a book;
Turned, said: 'You're no comfort to me.'

What about me?
'You? You do what you will.'
Was that some kind of joke?

You can ask this brook
What's meant to be, or not to be,
When it's had its fill.

THE MUSE

A voice came out of the green wall.
It said: 'I have you now –
Your attention, all of it, and so you.
I am nothing you *allow*.

I come at you, again, again.
Like what? Like bird cries, yes?
Then why am I the one whose skin is pecked
And bleeding? Why must I confess?

It was enough to see me once
Outside the Oosterpark.
I had my jacket hood up, but you saw
Enough to make the world go dark.

And so you fret at that, till all
The good it could have done
Unravels and lies waste: my ribbon roads
Converging on a zero-sun.

That's how you'd like me to put it.
The truth is, I was there
In body, and you passed me by; in spirit,
And all you dreamt of was my hair.

It's past now. That's the point for you.
Should I put make-up on
For that look poets love, so deathly pale?
It is me too, you know. I'm gone.'

ON A SUNDAY

Sundays were God, Country and Western music
On the radio, Mum ironing shirts for school
Listening-not-listening to Lena Martell
Sing 'I'm only human, and I'm a woman'
While I mooned about the place, tutting
In my grandfather shirt. What did I want
To happen? Well, nothing that *could* do, here.
Escape into books, into music (mine),
Into girls (one girl, never wholly mine):
The old familiar story. Different, how?
As different as it was – I was – to be
Lonely on a Sunday,
Tired to death of the thought of God,
Impatient for the Goddess to appear.

AMSTERDAM

1

Canal girdle. Right you are:
Constriction of a woman's body.
A pubic mound on the map.
I've lived in your soft belly
Three years, all told.
Why won't you sleep?
Perpetual orgasm's a fake.
Though in the cold daylight
I'll remember the love we've made,
Lieve dame, I'm longing
For emptier spaces, fewer
Lives at an end and happy.

2

And now I miss the winter sun
On the dark and moving body
Of canal water; miss the snow
Landing pell-mell in January.

Loosen your girdle a fraction:
I'm not the most dissolute guy
You ever accommodated.
There is some love you can't deny.

MICHIEL DE KONING'S 'M'

The original Dutch version of this poem-sequence
by Michiel de Koning (1930–2002) has never been published.
De Koning's own existence is confined to the unpublished
novel, *Femke*.

1

The hurt child who's mistaken for a sage
Will have the elders nodding in agreement
As they plot his death … Go, son, act your age:
Your mother's slip is not a priestly vestment.
Enamoured of the strength of the long-haired,
You've had your nose too long in that big book.
All who stopped there have, in the end, despaired:
You want to avoid their pinched, thin-lipped look.
It's not too late: the boats dance in the water,
The dandelion seed drifts on the breeze.
Squint at the sun – summers will not be hotter –
Or chase a ball with bruised and bloodied knees.
Don't fret, not in the slightest, about sin.
Ahead of you lies death, and Madeleine.

2

I am not my son. My son says: I am
Not my father. And yet I make the boy
(God forgive me) assume my martyrdom
At your hands. Madeleine, no silken joy
Runs through my grief that time has separate shores
On which to strand us. Long washed up, I see
You come into your own. My blue Azores
Match your Antillean isles to a T,
Save in age. (Every schoolboy understands
The need to tease the elders as they probe
In dark.) You even now reach out your hands,
Your hands that cast no dice and rent no robe,
But bring me hyacinths from the meadow
And put them in a vase, and set them so.

3

The sun and wind and all the planet's filth
Conspire to weather our extremities.
Some people, darkened by the heat of tilth
Or else a spot of gardening on their knees,
Scrub and scrub the dirt to their heart's content.
Your hand, so pale within the white, so pale
And gestureless, reminds me what was meant
By God when he made Adam firm and hale
With outstretched arm. Reject me, Madeleine,
And be a Muse to God. I'll only lie
To get my man's deserts, and call you mine,
And never once guess that you are lonely.
It's your pale hand in a white glove's mysterious;
Touched, and the dart of longing will be His.

4

You play a game. A game of memory.
What was the weather like when we first kissed?
How many tram stops to the brewery
Where your small flat was? (Does it still exist?)
Who spoke the word 'love' first? In which month? Where?
What was our first row about? Who invented
The curtain-signal?

               Love, I stroke your hair
And leave the answers that you crave unsaid,
Not because, as you suppose, I can't play
The game as well as you – let's be grown-up
About it – but because my memory
Is so strong, really so strong, it might rip
Us both to pieces. You think not? *Stormy,*
Six, you, May, Hollandsche Rading, her, me.

5

You came back when the gas was at a peep
And stared into my eyes as if you knew,
And, naturally, you did know. The steps were steep,
And you were breathless, still, and then you flew
And wounded me, quite rightly – first my head
And then my chest, my gut, lastly my groin –
And wept, and said you wished that I was dead
And then wished you were … I could only join
Your hands together, placing my own on top,
Whisper again the Malay word for milk
Which soothed you once before, till you said 'Stop,'
Unknotted the red ribbon of pure silk
And gave a better gift – your loosened hair
That's never greyed, through all your great despair.

6

There is an old, old woman made of stone
Watching over you, and at your window
She'll sign to the Black Rider you're alone
With a curtain's twitch. Then a man will mow
His lawn precisely at the point you scream.
I do not know the man. I know the woman:
I left her at a bridge inside a dream,
Since when she has aged terribly. My sin
Is not that you were murdered in my head
As a man in my own shoes stood idly by,
But that I let you lure me into bed
With that same trick I taught you – I, I, I.
Three twitches of the curtain, and I stepped
Into your lamplight while another slept.

7

As the cat eats wax from your ear-finger,
Symphony Orchestra Baden-Baden
Plays the Fifth. You look up. 'No high drama,'
You say, and curl back to your magazine
With that new-wife look certain men would kill for.
You're baffled by my air of absence-presence
(Which, happily, young doctors have a pill for).
Ah, but all's resolved with a major cadence:
I lie with you in many ways. None fails.
The cat's next door now, overturning something.
Downstairs a small girl practises her scales.
'I met the mother. Nice. No wedding ring.'
The days go by, the nights, an even pace.
You confiscate my Luger, just in case.

8

Madeleine, the word is out. Quick, let's go
And find some floor to lie on. Finish dressing
In the car (I'll drive). Oh love, don't be slow.
These rooms aren't safe now. Time is pressing.
And you can always come back by yourself
In a little while.

           Please, don't look at me
Like that. I'm not mad. Nothing's on the shelf
That we can't go without. Don't cry. You'll see,
In a little while, just how hopeless
It always was, our living in this city,
Where everything's permitted, nothing is.
They say the wolf's returning. There's a way
To live condemned with his air of being free
That we can't go without. Don't cry. You'll see.

9

This is the bread of exile, this the cup
With birds and blueberries, your favourite. Not
Austere enough? We can always make it up:
Rub our hands for warmth, drink from a tin pot –
Anything other than sit in this silence
Where shadows lengthen and diminish, and,
Before we're done, the bread basket's a fence,
The butter knife is spreading grains of sand
On slabs of slate. You miss the 'old us'. Yes,
I miss us too: quite nice people, we were.
Forget all that. Don't think of this as less –
It's not been given to us to 'prefer'.
We're in an altered world. A simple dish,
With bread beside, has everything we wish.

10

It's no life, not for you. I see that now.
Forgive me, love. And when you're done forgiving,
Forgive me still. A child who beat her brow
Against her wall at night knows well reliving
Terror is no life. Not for you. For me,
My part, I thought to take you in my arms,
Take you bodily somewhere you would be,
As the hymnist says, safe from all alarms –
A quiet summerhouse, some dear green place
Where the dragonfly whirrs uneven wings –
Would smooth away the terror from your face,
The terror I utterly can't bear.
                                    These things
You've seen I would not wish on any daughter.
Forgive me. I forgot how young you were.

11

In the studied brown air, old heads are smoking.
'What, pray, is the time value of money?'
The one with fish-eyes asks. He isn't joking,
And I can't tell yet if it's yesterday,
Or last year, or a century ago.
'I lost my love. The Black Rider took her.
Have you seen her? Or him?' The old heads know
On the bang of a gong it's time for supper;
Thick-jowled, they can still – briefly – salivate.
Menus are called for. A cipher fetches.
'Gentlemen, you are old. I am too late.
You cannot help me.' Old fish-eyes retches:
'The time value of money is the fear
Of losing what you've lost. No girl passed here.'

12

Here's how I found you, finally: foot in hand
And staring at the wall. 'A speck, a flaw,
The least thing bears most love. You understand?'
I didn't spare your feelings, still so raw.
'I hate all that. Don't want to lose desire.'
Your hurt look, non-serene, was like a kiss.
'Us, here,' I went on, 'that's real. Nothing's higher.'
After our exile, our return, your bliss
Was in another place. I couldn't get there,
However much I made out not to try.
That room you moved round by degrees: we met there,
You in black, with your long straight back, and I
Aghast that I had made you so still.
                                        Race
Towards me, love. I'm staring into space.

Night Singing

BIRTH

'You'll see
That bottom field flood in winter
And the swans come in.'

We take the word of a neighbour,
Twist it till it suits our need
And our son's come.

THE SEA

You forgot the sea –
You with your baby son, on a swing, happy –
Until some woman there meant company.
And so you moved, to where his eyes could see,
Carefully down steps turned seaweedy,
Thinking how we
Inherit memory
And carrying high your son who seemed happy
That you remembered the sea.

DAYS

I'm sorry now
I ever spurned the everyday,
Preferred to mirrors 'tragic pools',
As if the steady drip of days
Prepared a flood for us.

'Whatever happens happens in a day.'
Like this I soothe myself, supposing
You won't detect
My voice quivering when I read: *The wolf
Climbed into her warm bed and waited.*
'On what day?' So your eyes appear to say.

Son, nothing's safe.
Do you hear that? Do you see
A wolf, now, or passing woodsman
In me?

DEATH EXPLAINED

The crab was dead.
'Look at the crab!' I said,

My son asked, quietly,
'Is it waiting for somebody?'

THE PUPPET

I broke your puppet.
Can you fix it?
You've had it forever,
You say. I'm sorry.
To this day,
Dolls, puppets make me shiver.
(They can't die;
One day I'll die.)
I knew when I clapped eyes on it
I'd break your puppet.

SOFT PLAY

At Jumping Jacks
The kids can all go wild.
We're parked outside The Liquor Store,
Our young son softly snoring.

He'll wake when you're inside
And scream the car down, pound me with his fists.
I'll hold him, tell him no – as always,
Relishing the fight in him.

ETYMOLOGY OF WENT

'Yesterday I goed on a ferry-boat.'
'That's wrong, son,' I want not to say,
Want not to think mechanically,
Bad grammar, but you've learned the rule at least,
While you see again an island emerging.

In truth, I love your error. And I know
You're only stating simple fact
In a way that sounds colourful to me,
A father who would greyly mumble
'Went: from *wend*, grafted onto *go*.'

I'm cloaked in words, equating past with true.
All past is yesterday to you.

A BAD DREAM

You wake to shout: 'It's painted black!'
But I don't prod and probe to know
Your store of comic-book grotesques.
I let you turn back on your side.
Soft underbelly, royal highroad:
Why not just say the Land of Dreams,
And let the birds care what it is
And where it leads? (Tall, strutting birds.)
I want to keep you from the pain
Of knowing what I'm loth to tell:
That what we don't know hurts us most.

THE WORLD

'Get to bed. There's nothing to see.'
'You think there's nothing in the world.'

– No, son, I don't think that.
And though I knew a wise man once
Who said, 'The world's run by the dead,'
I'd like you to see more of it
Than this small patch of Ireland.

All right, I've met princesses,
Ambassadors and such,
And live as if in hiding;
But it might mean more to you, all that,
Or you might make better use of it
Than your old man has.
                    Don't look so
Forlorn as I close the curtains.
You know I only close them now
Because it's time to go to sleep.

THE LAST INSTRUCTION

After he's read – out loud – the last instruction
On a packet of porridge oats, my son
Frightens me with the prospect of my own
Deep-seated melancholy being passed on
To this still playful but too serious boy,
As he asks: 'Why do we have to *enjoy?*'

BENTHIC

I bought my son a Benthic Robot
From a quirky vintage toyshop in the heart of Brussels.
It was through absence-guilt of mine he got
To clutter shelves and windowsills.

Don't ask me now what they all were.
Those work-trip trinkets that were never really to his taste
Are gone, but for this wind-up deep-sea diver,
Unrusting, boxed and florid-faced.

It took a few steps, then keeled over,
And invalidity, like some oily preservative,
Has kept it good as new. No more a rover,
In my son's care I'd gladly live.

HAIR

That my hair,
As my mum said,
Was dirty fair
I never doubted.

She wasn't one
To gloat over
Feats of her son
Or praise failure.

What of my son,
And what is his?
I tell him: 'Golden.'
Golden it is.

TEETH

You're right, son, as you shake your toy and cry,
'It hasn't got teeth to say Cockatoo.'
For mind, an O-gape won't suffice.
But it's not nice
To dwell on flaws – or jaws – in one you love
(Even a bear who can't say Cockatoo).
How much more flawed I, the bad-toothed, would be
If not for you.

NO TIGERS

It's dark between the doors.
My son looks out: 'No tigers?
No tigers, no.'
That said, he is happy to go.

I have no such fears. I have no such tigers.

AFTER PLAYSCHOOL

'I was sad of you,' my young son says, meaning
He missed me. So we cherish each mistake
As once we cherished milestones – the long weaning,
First words and steps, all done for his own sake,
Yet prompting gratitude (ours, but to whom?).
Now do I say, 'I missed you too,' or, rather,
As I want to, checking who's in the room,
'And I was sad of you'? Pity the father
Who lacks recourse to memory to decide
What he should do and say. My dad died young,
And it was *de rigueur* at home to hide
Sorrow, leave love on the tip of the tongue ...
Forget it. I'll say what I want to my son.
'And I was sad of you. Did you have fun?'

THE HAIL

'If the hail falls in your hand it will die.'
If you ever fell silent I would die
And curl up in a ball,
Not to be here at all,
Like an old draft of a poem left to drift
Over a rubbish heap, nobody's gift;
Which advertised how I, still childless, felt;
On which the hail would melt.

MY SON'S WATCH

It is pure joy to take a heated blade
And make a hole in plastic for my son
So that his watch will fit him. It was done
Exactly so, I was exactly his age,
In those rough days when leather ruled the wrist
(It's burnt leather I remember). I had
Nothing to measure – time did not exist –
And only the example of my dad,
Whose watch stopped almost at the moment he did.

My son's watch has no hands to stop. I've made
The hole as neat, as far along as he
Could wish. (As I was, he's a slender boy.)
Why does it all – the hole, the heat, the blade –
Seem less a memory than a presage?
No, keep the dark at arm's length from this joy.

TIME

'Is tomorrow today?'
Son, I have the same
Fraught difficulty
With time. (Only, with me
It goes the other way.)
Though I tell you it's a shame
To wish away the day,
It's another day I see:

And not thoughts of a party
I lose this moment for;
Not your look of dismay
On seeing me forget
The point of the game we play.
Old loss makes me mutter,
To my own dismay,
'Is it yesterday yet?'

A CHILD'S COSMOLOGY

'The sun must kill the moon'
– So you say,
But I don't know
If that's a child's cosmology
Or just a joke. We go
Along the mountain road to Sligo,
You in my rear-view mirror,
The sun a blur.
Me (call it my affliction),
I always sided with the moon.
Now you are my sun,
Can't we three
Live in harmony?

'The sun must kill the moon.'

LOGIC

1
'The moon's not safe.'
I never had that thought,
That the moon
Was at risk from night,
But you had,
With logic almost lunatic, and not
By moonlight alone.

2
We're watching the game
When there's a break in play:
A head wound
From which, unnervingly,
Blood flows down
In streams. 'I have blood too,' you say.
'Remember my blood.'

NOTHING

I had been not-listening to my son
The best part of a minute, on a walk
In the drizzling rain. And in the time
I dwelt on my substantial thoughts, his talk,
I grew to hear, was peppered with the word
Nothing. So many nothings, so much talk
Returning always to absence, extinction,
And not those things encountered on a walk –
Crows cawing from the elms, whatever else
He missed because his mind was nothing-filled
And I because of my substantial thoughts –
Which scattered soon enough, leaving me thrilled
By his ambition at the edge of town:
'To walk on nothing, and never fall down.'

UNANSWERED

What is God what is eyeballs what is forehead?
– I can no more answer your fevered question
Than I can pay a visit to the dead
And ask my own dad where they bury the sun
Each night, and who *they* are, and what's the sense
That hears light in a smell touched by the tongue.
And when they put the razor on the wire,
Do they really mean to injure the young?
And what's TRESPASS? And is there any land
Unknown, and can I go? And if he bled
Much, and how a wolf can know the time, and
What is God what is eyeballs what is forehead?

THE WAIT

We waited for you
So long,
And now you're here.
You're here at last.

You're here –
Our wait is over,
Our wait that went on
So long.

But you're here now,
That's all that matters;
Here with us.
You're here at last.

NIGHT SINGING

There comes a time in singing to a child,
As the small limbs go limp and the breaths deepen,
That you become aware of weight. It's then
You hear your voice, and in it something wild.
Why do fears come? Nothing on any shelf
Can tell you in this place of simple rhyme.
The child's asleep, and has been for some time.
You're only singing now to soothe yourself.

TOWNIES

'I'm jumping,' she says, 'in the muddle puddles.'
She's on 'a walk' – pink wellies, red coat – meaning
I'll carry her half the way.
                                           'This is moss.
Touch it. It's all right.' 'Can I touch this leaf?'
'Yes.' 'Is it fresh?' 'It's green, that means it's fresh.' 'Ow!'
'Oh, sorry. Roses will grow on that bush.'

There's the small tractor again, almost toylike.
A hobby farm, perhaps. They spring up here,
As folks blow in, like us, with fresh pretension –
Like raising kids in safety, close to nature.

'That's the farmer's,' she says, looking round for one.
Then, eyes closing, she cries: 'The farmer's gone!'
I tell her he'll be in his house, not looking
Or saying what I think: *His house in Dublin.*
It seems to work. She perks up. 'There's the farmer!'

My smile at her invention hasn't faded
When I see it – the face she sees, sneering,
Hogging the shed window. 'Hullo! Hullo!'

She squirms under my hands to let her down
And run to the car. We go back to town.

An Attic Room
on Rose Street

LANDSCAPE

I draw my hands apart
So you're free to go.
The blue trees rise again:
This landscape I know.

EVERYTHING AND NOTHING

The tall candles I was taught to keep
For Last Rites in a papered drawer –
These were the twin gates of sleep
You burned for pleasure.

'Everything's permitted,' you said,
'Not just to us, to everyone.
Maybe not in the books you've read,
But in this one.'

Nothing I had was not yours.
You were that woman by Picasso
Soothing with a whisper, with slender fingers
Me, your crow.

SMOKE

Blue smoke from a cigarette,
But the mouth's smoke is grey.
They ascend, the blue singularly
Pure and true and straight,

The grey shapeless, cloudy, yet
Human, somehow, too —
Or let us say my faults make you
The purer of us two …

The room fills with two colours.
Tired of the analogy,
He sees that both the blue and grey
Are his, neither's hers.

LOOK!

Yes, yes, I killed Jocasta in my sleep.
It's wrong, I know. If I get up, I'll see
Astonishing sunlight on your garden.
But eyes tear fistfuls of grass in a frenzy
Because this dream won't leave me.

We meet on the steps, your cigarette
Held in bleeding hand. You look lost to me.
I think suddenly, *The red curtain*!
Its cloth kingfisher flown from the tree
To peck at you blindly.

THE OLD GROUND

Had you with me, I knew.
And going over the old ground,
The old moon-connected ground –
Earth I'd avoided, as if
Inertia could stave off disaster
Long enough – reached a place
This side of the pylons:
Trees like young women, elongated trees.

Were these the selfsame trees
I'd stood next to, unalone,
A hand covering my face
Like Harlequin, blocking out the town?
Examined branches (as though we could string
Trauma, warmth, dependence, need,
The whole caboodle of childhood,
Delicately through those trees) …

'Dead, but in a good way,' you said.

AS YOU MOVED

It was too soon to expose them,
When your insomnia shone like frost –
Hidden things, for them to see the sun.
And so my past fell from me;
So my expression melted in the sun.

Then, with a sleep-walker's nonchalance,
Dressed not in mother-blue but brown,
After an autumn, winter and spring,
After our separation,
You met me at the heart of town.

And only the jackal could have stood beside us,
Could have moved across the steps like you,
As you moved towards me then,
Over the wide stair,
Over the wide, stone, crumbling stair.

THE SNOWY ROAD

The snowy road preserved my fear,
My longed-for town defined itself through drifts
In masts, in spires, in railings,
And everything began again, not least the heart.

Speak my name as I speak yours,
In snow-dishevelled country:
I walked out that way, know all the roads.

US

Nothing rolls across the space.
Perhaps a Catherine Wheel can light it
Fitfully, a few seconds,
Enough to make out faces;
Enough, but not enough, to make out us.

You're always night, a house
Which suddenly grows steeper.
I think I can step into you.
I surround myself with you.
You're like September air, cooling, true.

It's years ago I saw you
Step out from a train —
Seven years, then this day.
Not red or mother-blue, your dress;
A vision, less the suffering.
                              Her light is,
   Catherine's, going now, goodbye.

FOR WINTER

I thought my love for winter lost
Till your insomniac eyes of frost
Burned into me, so pure and clear
With slow abandonment of fear.

LOOKS

Dog-tired, harassed,
Still you manage a look
Of Spanish Rose.

I'm haunted by your look
Of barely hours ago.

EVENING

I heard you the first time
Say 'Careful as you go,'
But could not keep my feet,
And went down in the snow.

So, overwhelmed by snow,
I laughed to see you keen,
Until only the moon
And one star could be seen.

AT BREAKFAST

And parachuting down the vast aerodrome,
Your dream's manikins. Lost, I lose the gist;
At breakfast, bite down hard
As though to get at meaning through a capsule.

Did I somehow give rise to them?

Those nothings, faces blank and unattending.

ESCAPE

1

A woman died one day
In a vile village, alone
(Her beckoning finger
Had scared all away).
Why did I think we could
Ever be like her, live
Where softly sagging wood
Tells truly all subsides?

2

Escape's
The word on everybody's lips,
And we're no different:
Our life's in the sticks.
We like the isolation;
We never reminisce.
And yet I know
You sometimes wonder
How long we can be left to play like this.

MY BEST

It was the nearest thing to love;
At least, a declaration of it –
'All you can do is your best,
You can't do any more than that':
A certain filial regard
Not contingent upon success;
Mere parroting of something said.
The words would fail on entering
Examination hall or office
Where I sat trussed up to be grilled.

What was my best? Nothing any
Invigilator oversaw,
Examiner gave credit for,
Or interviewer cared to know.
None put me at my ease as you
Or was near half as exacting.
I've never had to memorise
The date we met or how you looked
Or what I felt that day. It's you:
The best of me, all I can do.

HEAT AND COLD

'You're never cold,' you say. And I'm rebuked
For not being keen on one last blast of heat.
'But summer's barely gone,' I want to say
Less cagily, remembering Septembers –
Those solitary rain-soaked walks to school.
I'm never cold, I think, swelling with pride
(As when, one lonely joyless night, you came
Back late, with wine-breath sweetly answering
My 'How was it?' and unspoken 'without me?',
'Oh, you know, no show without Punch.'). 'That's not,'
I answer, 'a bad way to be.' And you:
'I wanted someone to be cold *with* me.'

THE WAY IT IS

I need to keep you close,
As skin to bone,
As ear to the receiver.
Though if you stray, there's always
The tumbler full of whisky;
That song about the farm.
And it's because of you
I can't be satisfied
Unless my pulse is racing.
And it's because of you
I battle longing
For pulse and all to cease.

BUILDINGS

We found them quite desirable
In a clean, open-to-the-outside way –
The new-builds near the Texaco.
I pictured sometime-weds, their kids at play,
Retired folk watchful at windows;
Was startled by a real face staring back;
Walked on, aware now of our shadows.
'What's that up there?' I felt your hand go slack,
You edge ahead. It was a building
Not fully screened from view, ivied and tall.
We crossed some softer ground to read
The State-green plaque. A 'fever hospital'.
And now the whole scene opened up –
The graveyard; benches for the Famine tourist;
Angular, ill-judged public art.
Was it here local, dark-souled lovers kissed?
We stayed looking at the bleak building
('Where to now?' 'Don't know. You decide.')
As if it were the kind of Gothic
That we like, that we'd like to live inside.

TEMPER

I'll rein in my temper,
My confused self saying, 'Love me,
Even at times like these,'
Because I want to grow
As the nasturtiums grow
On our sill, each tendril
Adept at finding light, more and more light.

REVOLUTIONS

Revolutions start on railway platforms;
Also love. For us, platform fourteen,
Edinburgh Waverley. And afterwards
A photo exhibition. You turned green –

Or so I thought, or so I liked to think –
As I stood, just a bit too long, before
A sultry Jodie Foster wearing red.
We drew close, closer passing through the door,

And crossed the road into an altered world:
The daunting facades didn't fly apart,
And all was not suddenly smoking ruins,
Pistol shots, bodies slumped in a hand-cart.

Still, it felt different, in those Georgian streets,
As we looked up and saw the sky clearing,
And arranged when next to meet, two strangers
Loving at first sight, touch, taste, smell, hearing.

THE KEY

Why am I like this?
Some word that I forgot
Turned out to be the key
That could have opened all to me.
And here I am again,
After you said 'No more',
The selfsame empty-handed thief
At your door.

SAVED

You came back to my riverside,
Dull-as-ditchwater flat, and then,
Checking the urge to run and hide,
You saved me on my bed again.

The heron I'd thought gone for good
Was wading just below the window:
Less, now, the mark of solitude
Than a part of the river's flow.

The world can go to hell, and will.
I love you for your nakedness
That you made partly visible
Then put away beneath your dress.

B&B

'Fortuitous,' hissed the landlady.
One double left, so late at night:
Where was the fortune there? For me
It was in you, in your eyes bright
With youth, and longing. We had spent
The day in that sun-gilded town,
Following where the river went
– To this hall-hovering, snooty frown.

We were new lovers, wandering
The world and unafraid of all
Landladies with their laundering,
Their fake-gilt frames upon the wall.
We saw instantly through the fuss
A bed made for the two of us.

198/6 ROSE STREET

Across the street from Dirty Dick's
We lay under a leaking window
No hands, not even yours, could fix.
Rain soused the duvet, soused the pillow.

This hatched, in my head, dream-insects
Diaphanous enough to show
The same swirling, perfect defects
Of marbles played with long ago.

Love bears all, but nothing predicts
What love will find to love, and so
I see from out here in the sticks
An attic room on Rose Street glow.

THE QUARRY

We used to walk round to the quarry –
That arid wasteland near the beach.
Dust over all. We weren't sorry
To have destruction within reach.

Not that we were drawn to the dark,
Just that we felt a kind of beauty
In what was uniformly stark.
We were lovers. It was our duty.

The tight conveyor didn't spill,
Whirred on unmanned. You made the grey
Cohere around a red capsule
We knelt beside, as if to pray.

(It was an object made by you
And placed in that place for effect.
A quarryman appeared on cue,
Helped mount it with bemused respect.)

'Nature alive with industry' –

The sort of thing I might have said –
Is wrong. You taught me how to see,
But we had both long had our dead.

Although as green as anyone
Young and in love, we knew the same
Strange calm that comes when all's been done
To smash us up, with none to blame.

At times there were soft explosions
From the quarry. We used to walk
The coastal path through thorns and whins:
In the dead air, no aftershock.

THEN AND THEN

Ten years ago
You married me
In a Dutch church
Whose name translates
As 'chalk hill'.

And I think back
To a time I stood
At a blackboard, alone,
White chalk in hand,
My mind a blank.

I was what? Four?
Your moving finger,
Long, chalk-white,
Writes: You're not alone
Any more.

TO A TREE

Equal probability tree,
You are binomially we.

Starting with our end,
You work back to where we were,
To our initial node –
Factually, the Green Tree
On a bank-holiday Monday –
Always valuing where we've been,
Who we were at each step.
You know our underlying
Volatility better
Than we do ourselves,
Or we wouldn't be crying on the bed –
As each, by the other, has been found.
No matter our ups and downs –
Those *us* and *ds* – like you
We recombine.

Ah, no, dear tree. We don't believe in you.
(That pub in the Cowgate's gone too.)
At expiration,
The last sigh will be ours and ours
Alone.

FOOTFALL

I want to see your bare feet going downstairs.
It would be all I need to make the day
Begin in glory – the soft flesh, the skin
At stretch, covering the cuneiform bones.
Not that alone, the glory being in both
What's revealed, what's hidden: dorsum and planum.
You don't float down to me, but by degrees
Of articulated movement come, all woman –
And why stop short of saying Goddess-like,
With nothing to suggest a crucifixion
Immanent in the flesh? Carpeted now,
The stairs muffle, don't silence, your footfall.
Yet still it's not enough. I want to see
Your feet in their bare glory going downstairs.

A RIVER, LOVE

I have stepped into the same river twice.
You were there both times, were both times the same,
Not quite surefooted on the stepping stones;
Just as you were when I first spoke your name

– Whispering it, in my room again, alone.
That double-edged river ran quietly
Past the housefront. We watched it from the window
The next time you came.

                                    Now you turn and say:

'There is such tallness in my family,'
Wondering if our three could be as tall
As we watch them run. This much water's flowed.
And so, as the night traffic starts to crawl

In a city long left behind, we stare
At the window-framed mountain peak above
The town we've settled into, still the same
Two people joined by time, a river, love.

THE RED GARDEN

1
In that disused garden belonging to no one
You found an iron cage the size of two hands,
Shaped almost like a lantern,
And leant against a blue board in the fence.
The patterned sunlight moved into place.

2
No, we were never children
Playing in this garden.

Let me wrestle with you, angel,
Till I learn your defiant smile.

3
As in a dream,
You offered something –
Cicatrix, crucifix.
I was feeling along a wall for my wounds.

4
In the red garden
Kingfishers flew out of the moon.
A song went through my head at breakfast.
You were young.

5
You were crawling on the verge
Of being creature-like
On the brown, grassy slope.
The earth was hungry that day.
Not where the thorn-trees were,
Nearer.

6
I want you in an old light,
I want you there
In a past – my past – we didn't share,
The age you are.

Standing one foot on the pond's rim
Where I contemplated the swan,
Watched suicide move through him,
Waved him gone;

Holding, in the death-heavy room,
Slides of foreign cities –
My Athens, my Jerusalem:
My mind's deep-freeze.

7

Glass lifts; my tears
That normally'd transfix you;
Calling after you your name,
Your precious name, in the white arcade,
The presents tumbling from your arms:
None of these, nothing, nothing,
Turned your head in the dream.

Sister in an adjoining room
Sucking you back into time …

Turn, just once, your head in the dream.

8

Horses were an unknown; slept sound
In the next field.
Morning showed the gap.
'They might have trampled us.'
No, they're kinder, horses.
Horses stand for my father.

We dressed lying down, collapsed the tent,
Stared at tree trunks:
They were forming a letter,
Bending towards us, one another, leaning
To cross and recross – was it M, like Rilke's '*M*,
Standing for Mothers'?

9

The back of your ear is so soft, you said.
Harvest moon, when no one's home.

10

It feels strange again,
And sometimes sleep intervenes:
Our wires uncross,
Bodies stretch.
If bed can be an ocean,
As I've seen it said,
It can be any landscape:
You crawling through rough grass,
I examining
All those roads in the dark I'm drawn to.
It feels strange
That night should be so tender.
I never knew.